utb 2997

Eine Arbeitsgemeinschaft der Verlage

Böhlau Verlag · Wien · Köln · Weimar
Verlag Barbara Budrich · Opladen · Toronto
facultas · Wien
Wilhelm Fink · Paderborn
A. Francke Verlag · Tübingen
Haupt Verlag · Bern
Verlag Julius Klinkhardt · Bad Heilbrunn
Mohr Siebeck · Tübingen
Nomos Verlagsgesellschaft · Baden-Baden
Ernst Reinhardt Verlag · München · Basel
Ferdinand Schöningh · Paderborn
Eugen Ulmer Verlag · Stuttgart
UVK Verlagsgesellschaft · Konstanz, mit UVK/Lucius · München
Vandenhoeck & Ruprecht · Göttingen · Bristol
Waxmann · Münster · New York

StandardWissen Lehramt

Die Bände zur Didaktik des Englischen werden herausgegeben von Engelbert Thaler

Bisher sind erschienen:

A. Müller-Hartmann/M. Schocker-v. Ditfurth: Teaching English: Task-Supported Language Learning
J.-U. Keßler/A. Plesser: Teaching Grammar
K. Heim/M. Ritter: Teaching English: Computer-assisted Language Learning
E. Thaler: Teaching English with Films

Engelbert Thaler

Teaching English Literature

2., aktualisierte Auflage

Ferdinand Schöningh

Der Autor:

Engelbert Thaler, Prof. Dr. phil. habil., ist Professor für die Didaktik des Englischen an der Universität Augsburg. Nach dem Lehramtsstudium arbeitete er 20 Jahre als Gymnasiallehrer für Englisch und Sozialkunde. Er habilitierte sich an der Ludwig-Maximilians-Universität München über offene Lernarrangements im Fremdsprachenunterricht. Seine Publikationen befassen sich neben literaturdidaktischen Themen u.a. mit mediendidaktischen Zugängen (Musikvideoclips im Englischunterricht, Film Based Language Learning), unterrichtsmethodologischen Fragen (Balanced Teaching) und kulturkundlichen Aspekten (Fußball in Forschung und Fremdsprachenunterricht, Popular Culture). Thaler ist auch Herausgeber von Schulbüchern, Fachzeitschriften und Unterrichtsreihen.

Online-Angebote oder elektronische Ausgaben sind erhältlich unter **www.utb-shop.de**

Bibliografische Information der Deutschen Nationalbibliothek
Die Deutsche Nationalbibliothek verzeichnet diese Publikation in der Deutschen Nationalbibliografie; detaillierte bibliografische Daten sind im Internet über http://dnb.d-nb.de abrufbar.

2., aktualisierte Auflage

(Verlag Ferdinand Schöningh GmbH & Co. KG, Jühenplatz 1, D-33098 Paderborn)

Internet: www.schoeningh.de

Printed in Germany
Einbandgestaltung: Atelier Reichert, Stuttgart auf Grundlage eines Entwurfes von Alexandra Brand und Judith Karwelies
Layout: Alexandra Brand und Judith Karwelies

UTB-Band-Nr: 2997
ISBN 978-3-8252-4515-3

Vorwort zur Reihe

StandardWissen Lehramt – Studienbücher für die Praxis

Wie das gesamte Bildungswesen wird sich auch die künftige Lehramtsausbildung an Kompetenzen und Standards orientieren. Damit rückt die Frage in den Vordergrund, was Lehrkräfte wissen und können müssen, um ihre berufliche Praxis erfolgreich zu bewältigen. Das Spektrum reicht von fachlichen Fähigkeiten über Diagnosekompetenzen bis hin zu pädagogisch-psychologischem Wissen, um Lehren als Unterstützung zur Selbsthilfe und Lernen als eigenaktiven Prozess fassen zu können.

Kompetenzen werden nicht in einem Zug erworben; Lehrerbildung umfasst nicht nur das Studium an einer Hochschule, sondern ebenso das Referendariat und die Berufsphase. Die Reihe StandardWissen Lehramt bei UTB bietet daher Lehramtsstudierenden, Referendaren, Lehrern in der Berufseinstiegsphase und Fortbildungsteilnehmern jenes wissenschaftlich abgesicherte Know-How, das sie im Rahmen einer neu orientierten Ausbildung wie auch später in der Schule benötigen. Fachdidaktische und pädagogisch-psychologische Themen werden gleichermaßen in dieser Buchreihe vertreten sein – einer Basisbibliothek für alle Lehramtsstudierenden, Referendare, Lehrerinnen und Lehrer.

Contents

GENRES

ABOUT LITERATURE

Introduction | 0

Reading and literature play an important part in people's lives – and that should be reflected in the English language classroom. Christine Nuttall may be right when claiming that "reading is like an infectious disease – it is caught, not taught". But teachers can create the virus and, by providing a literature-rich environment, make it grow.

Intention and structure

This book intends to help teachers in pursuing this task. As it is an introduction, it aims to look at all the main areas of teaching English literature in a user-friendly way, but does not dig too deeply into each field. English literature does not only mean the literature of England or the British Isles, but all literature written in the English language. The book consists of four parts, comprising 12 chapters, so that university teachers may – if they wish to – devote one weekly meeting to each chapter, covering the whole contents in one term. The first part (*basis*) tries to answer the questions of what literature is and why, when, where, and what for it should be taught in foreign language classrooms. The second part discusses the *competences* that our students should develop in literature classes (knowledge, skills, attitudes). The main *genres*, i.e. novels, plays, poems and also short narrative forms, are the focus of the third part. The final part goes further, exploring the relationship between literature and modern media and discussing ways of assessing students' LCC (literary communicative competence).

New type of textbook

This book gives its adressees a brief and reader-friendly introduction to a new field of study. A didactically reflected structure, several graphical elements, concentration on the essential aspects, and a – hopefully – clear style aim at giving the reader a quick and comprehensive survey of the new field. It is written for university students (and their teachers), practising teachers and everybody interested in helping young people to want to read.

In this book every chapter starts with an awareness-raising, pre-reading question, which often makes readers reflect on their own personal experiences, since teacher development and reflective teaching need to take the (future) teacher's learning biography into account. Moreover this book contains a lot of sample texts, which illustrate the argumentation and may stimulate the readers to try them out in their classes. The lesson plans for various levels are meant to serve the same purposes.

Basis

1 Literature: What?

1.1 Definitions

How would you distinguish between a literary and a non-literary text?

What is literature?

"What is literature?" This question by the great French philosopher Jean-Paul Sartre has not been answered satisfactorily yet, although countless literary theorists have tried to do so. Everybody seems to have an intuitive understanding of the term *literature*. Yet to be able to make a distinction between literary and non-literary texts, one needs some reliable categories.

Functions of language

A good starting-point may be the outstanding Russian linguist ROMAN JAKOBSON. Based on the six dimensions he postulates for the communication process, he distinguishes between six functions of language.

Functions of language

Dimension	*Function*	*Explanation*
Addresser	Emotive, expressive	To convey one's attitude towards the addressee (self-expression)
Addressee	Conative	To influence the attitudes of the addressee (persuasive addressing of recipient)
Message	Poetic	To refer reflexively to the form of the message (autotelic: having itself as its purpose)
Subject	Referential	To relate the message to reality (contextual information)
Contact	Phatic	to establish contact between addresser and addressee (channel of communication)
Code	Metalingual	To refer to the linguistic code (checking code working)

Based on Jakobson's communication model, Nünning/Nünning developed a model of literary communication (2004:13). An author (addresser) produces a literary text (message), using the medium of writing (channel), and sending it to the reader (addressee, recipient). To understand the text, which – in aesthetically mediated form – refers to the historical and contemporary reality (context), the reader and the author must share a common language and some background knowledge (code). Several institutions (publishers, media, critics) act as mediators of literary works.

Model of literary communication

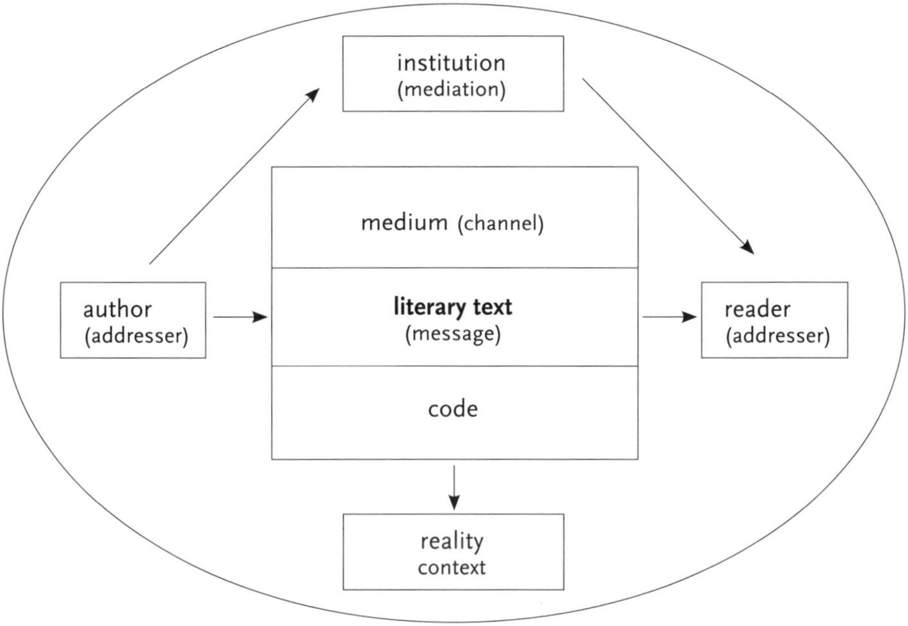

Models like this put the literary text into a wider communicative context, but do not define what constitutes literature. Descriptive and normative definitions of literature can be found in encyclopaedia, e.g. the Random House Dictionary lists seven different aspects:

Definitions of literature

1. writings in which expression and form, in connection with ideas of permanent and universal interest, are characteristic or essential features, such as poetry, novels, history, biography, and essays
2. the entire body of writings of a specific language, period, people, etc.: *the literature of England*

3. the writings dealing with a particular subject: *the literature of ornithology*
4. the profession of a writer or author
5. literary work or production
6. any kind of printed material, such as circulars, leaflets, or handbills: *literature describing company products*
7. *Archaic.* polite learning; literary culture; appreciation of letters and books

Broad and narrow definitions

This definition already suggests that one can distinguish between broad and narrow definitions of literature (GRABES 1981). In the broadest sense, literature comprises all forms of written communication, i.e. written, printed works. British literary histories such as the The Oxford History of English Literature, for example, also include essays, travel literature, pamphlets as well as semi-fictional or non-fictional text types like biographies and works of philosophy. Narrower definitions reduce the scope by focussing on various criteria, very often referring to the poetic and imaginative quality of literary texts. The criteria used, however, are subject to historic change and vary from one cultural context to another.

Literature with a capital *L* and a small *l*

Against the background of broad and narrow definitions, McRae (1997) made a distinction between *Literature with a capital L* and *literature with a small l*. Whereas the former consists of the classical texts of English literatures, such as those by Shakespeare, Dickens, Austen, the latter includes jokes, puns, graffiti, advertisements, newspaper headlines and other short forms not commonly cherished as 'great' works. McRae's distinction encourages the teacher to use texts which may not be of outstanding aesthetic quality ('high-brow' literature), but are motivating because they are short, easy or funny.

Reality and ambiguity

Two recurring criteria for differentiating between literary and non-literary texts are the relation of a text to reality and its ambiguity (polyvalence). In contrast to 'referential texts', "literature makes no claim to convey or represent 'facts'" (Nünning/Nünning 2004: 16). The 'fictionality' (Latin *fingere*, to invent, form) of a text means that the setting (time, place, circumstances) and characters have been fabricated in the author's mind. Therefore literary texts cannot be judged as 'true' or 'false', but rather ask the reader to accept this invented world (*willing suspension of disbelief*: Samuel Taylor Coleridge). And contrary to the explicitness and clarity of non-fictional texts, literary texts "allow for various interpretations, thanks to their internal ambiguities" (Nünning/Nünning 2004: 18). If a text has several potential meanings, teachers cannot insist on a single, binding interpretation, and readers / pupils are offered enough freedom to construct their own meanings and interpretations.

1.2 Classifications

What genres of literature do you know?

Criteria for classifications

Classifications are a helpful tool to structure and order the vast amount of texts. Some of the most important criteria for categorising literature in English (and other languages) are listed in the table below. It goes without saying that the boundaries between the various categories are fluid.

Literature in the English language	
Nation	English, Scottish, Irish, American, US-American, Canadian, Australian, Indian, African etc.
Historical period	Medieval, Elizabethan, Augustan, Romantic, Victorian etc.
Sociological	Working-class, women's literature
Age	Children's literature, young adult fiction
Genre	Lyric, narrative, dramatic texts
Aesthetic evaluation	High-brow vs low-brow literature, avant-garde, popular literature, pulp fiction
Sense of production	Written, oral
Mode of writing	Narrative, descriptive, argumentative, expository, dramatic, satirical
Media	Printed text, oral literature, audio books, audiovisual, interactive formats, web-based
Relation to reality	Realistic (mimetic) vs fantasy (anti-mimetic) literature
Conventionality	Traditional, experimental, innovative literature

Genres One of the most influential and helpful categories of these is genre. Genres are "constructs based on socio-cultural, literary and social consensus" (VOSSKAMP 1992: 256) and are characterized by "generic features", i.e. special characteristics to do with content, form, and function. An overview of literary genres with two levels, starting with the three main types (lyric, narrative, dramatic genres), is suggested by the following tree diagram.

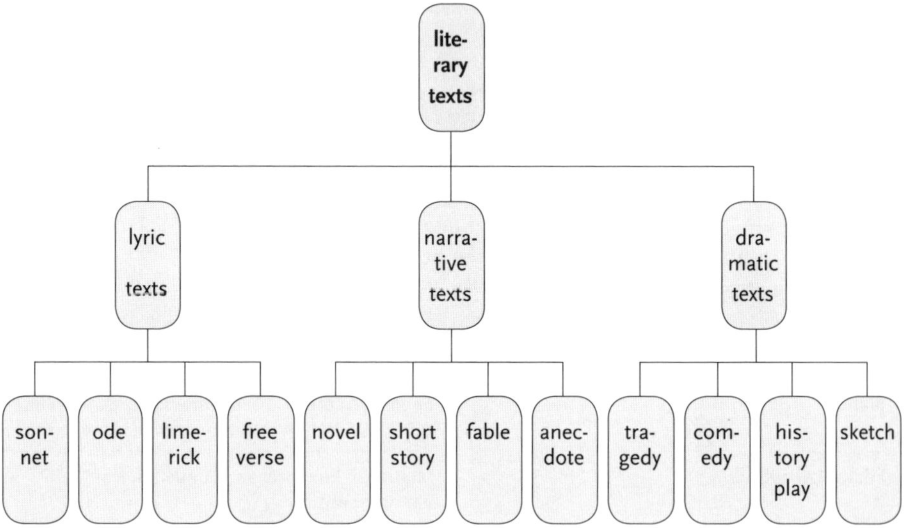

1.3 Selection

According to what criteria are you going to choose a text for your class?

The 3 C's When reading literature in class, the first and foremost task is to select a suitable work of literature for one's learners. The students' motivation and the efficiency of the learning process depend to a large extent on the right choice of literature. The three C's – catalogue, canon, criteria – can help in this important matter of selection.

Catalogues All publishing companies offer catalogues and brochures in which they inform the reading public about the books they have in stock. The publishers specialising in English language titles usually list their books according to age or reading ability. They include short descriptions about the book, and browsing through these pages can give the teacher a lot of new ideas.

Canon

A canon is a list of books which are generally recognized as being the most important pieces of literature – artistically superior examples known as classics. The English and American departments of many universities offer such canons on their homepages (e.g. Ludwig-Maximilians-Universität München: http://www.anglistik.uni-muenchen.de). In England, Education Secretary Alan Johnson and the Qualifications and Curriculum Authority (QCA) issued a list of recommended authors for the secondary curriculum in 2007:

QCA list of classic authors

Jane Austen, Elizabeth Barrett Browning, William Blake, Charlotte Bronte, Robert Burns, Geoffrey Chaucer, Kate Chopin, John Clare, Samuel Taylor Coleridge, Charles Dickens, Arthur Conan Doyle, George Eliot, Thomas Gray, Thomas Hardy, John Keats, John Masefield, Alexander Pope, Christina Rossetti, William Shakespeare (sonnets), Mary Shelley, Robert Louis Stevenson, Jonathan Swift, Alfred Lord Tennyson, HG Wells, Oscar Wilde, Dorothy Wordsworth and William Wordsworth.

Such canons may serve as a guideline and a contribution to a well-rounded (British) education, but they also pose problems because it is hard to find a consensus on which works to include, and some people reject its prescriptive, imperative quality. Moreover, the QCA list met with sharp criticism from teachers' organisations, who argued that teaching texts of such linguistic complexity to 11-14-year-olds, who are not yet ready for them, would be counter-productive and turn them off from classic authors. How much more complex must those classics seem to teenagers who learn English as a foreign language?

Criteria

A third source of selection can be used by looking at certain criteria. The following list contains some of the most important guidelines grouped around school, teacher, learner and text.

Criteria of Selection	
school	• type of school • level (primary, secondary)
learner	• age • level of proficiency • subjective valence (*Betroffenheit*) • interests • background
teacher	• personal favourites • study background • competences
text	• availability of text • linguistic difficulty • thematic complexity • literary genre • curricular conformity • length • aesthetic quality • topicality • popularity • methodological material (lesson plans, worksheets, analyses) • text-related media (film adaptations, audio books, websites) • exploitability for language learning (skills, competences)

Children's literature

Taking the age and the limited language proficiency of our students into consideration, the process of selection should pay special attention to three genres. As TEFL has been extended into the primary classroom, children's literature is a suitable genre for our young learners (Hunt 1996, Huck 2001). Fairy tales and other stories with strong repetitive elements are text types which our children are familiar with from their L1, and so they can focus on the language features more easily.

Young adult fiction

Young adult fiction has experienced a boom since the 1960s. The protagonists are teenage boys and girls, with whom young adults or adolescents can identify, and the stories are centred around issues that are relevant during puberty. In contrast to so-called *simplified readers*, they are authentic novels or plays, but language and style are not too elaborate so that they can be read from lower secondary classes (Bushman/Bushman 1997, Hesse 2002).

learner texts

If we take modern approaches like reader response theory seriously, we also have to include the learners' own texts. Whether they write e-mail texts, add a stanza to a pop song, review a film, or create their own poem – not only the great works of the classical authors are worth studying in a truly learner-centred classroom.

teacher and students as co-decision-makers

A good approach to selecting a literary work is to combine teacher initiative and student decision. The teacher pre-selects a certain number of books (3 – 6), which he regards as suitable for his group. Each book is introduced briefly, so that the learners know what to expect – without giving away too much. This can be done in a student-centred way by asking student groups (or single students) to prepare a short presentation. Finally the vote is taken, and the majority in class decide which book to read in detail.

Tasks

1. Decide whether the following examples belong to *Literature with a capital L* or *literature with a small l.*

– Shakespeare drama – pop song lyrics – sketch – Dickens novel – Beckett play – graffiti – limerick – Wordsworth poem – joke – Hemingway short story – anecdote – simplified/graded reader – young adult fiction – hard-boiled detective story – Bukovsky poem	**Literature with a capital *L*** .... **literature with a small *l*** ....

2. Have a look at the tree diagram of genres and find one example of English literature each for the 12 sub-genres on the second level.
3. Imagine you are a teacher in grade 10 (year 16). Choose a literary text and, guided by the list of selection criteria, decide whether you can use it in your class.

2 Literature: Why? When? Where? What for?

2.1 Rationale

Is it really necessary to use literary texts in class?

6 arguments for teaching literature

Why should people read and study literature? And why should teachers teach literature to EFL students? Various literary scholars and methodologists keep on pointing to the following reasons (e.g. Nuttall 1982, Collie/Slater 1987, Duff/Maley 1990).

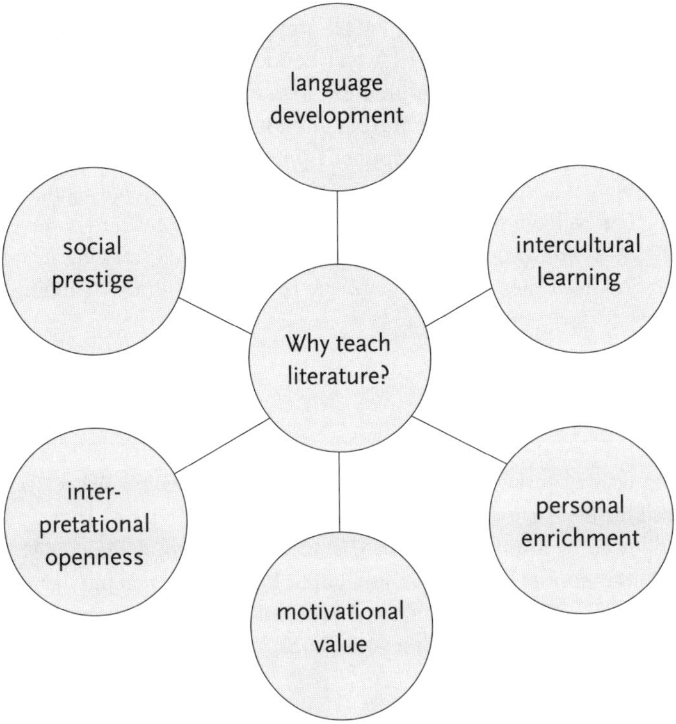

Integrating literature into the EFL classroom supports language learning, as literary texts are genuine samples of a wide range of styles and text types at all levels of difficulty. Thus the basic skills and competences (reading, speaking, writing, listening, mediating) and linguistic domains (lexis, grammar, pragmatics) can be improved (*language development*). Reading books from other countries opens the window to the world and may contribute to mutual understanding between the members of different cultures (*intercultural learning*). Learners may also profit from books as an individual, as they often touch on themes to which they can bring an individual response from their own experiences. They can open up new horizons, pose vital questions, offer different views of life, provide (positive or negative) role models, sketch possible answers to personally relevant issues (*personal enrichment*). If carefully chosen, a literary text means a welcome change from the everyday classroom routine, raising interest and suspense (*motivational value*). Due to its polyvalence, a literary text is open to multiple interpretation, which means that very rarely will two readers' understanding of a text be identical. This opinion gap between one's own interpreation and another's can be bridged by interaction. Thus literature demands a personal involvement and asks for individual responses (*interpretational openness*). Finally literature holds a high status in society (*social prestige*).

Example

The following excerpt is taken from Frank McCourt's novel *Teacher Man* (2005, chapter 1, pp. 19 – 21). While reading it, try to find examples of the six arguments for reading (and teaching) literature.

Example

Frank McCourt was 66 when his first book, *Angela's Ashes*, was published – a memoir about his childhood in Ireland. That was followed by another memoir, *'Tis*. In *Teacher Man: A Memoir* McCourt recounts his 30 years as a public high school teacher in New York City, giving memorable and humorous insights into the teaching profession – a valuable guide-book for every (future) teacher.

Mea culpa.

Instead of teaching, I told stories.
Anything to keep them quiet and in their seats.
They thought I was teaching.
I thought I was teaching.

I was learning.
And you called yourself a teacher?
I didn't call myself anything. I was more than a teacher. And less. In the high school classroom you are a drill sergeant, a rabbi, a shoulder to cry on, a disciplinarian, a singer, a low-level scholar, a clerk, a referee, a clown, a counselor, a dress-code enforcer, a conductor, an apologist, a philosopher, a collaborator, a tap dancer, a politician, a therapist, a fool, a traffic cop, a priest, a mother-father-brother-sister-uncle-aunt, a bookkeeper, a critic, a psychologist, the last straw.
In the teacher's cafeteria veterans warned me, Son, tell 'em nothing about yourself, They're kids, goddam it. You're the teacher. You have a right to privacy. You know the game, don't you? The little buggars are diabolical. They are not, repeat not, your natural friends. They can smell it when you're going to teach a real lesson on grammar or something, and they'll head you off at the pass, baby. Watch 'em. Those kids have been at this for years, eleven or twelve, and they have teachers all figured out. They'll know if you're even thinking about grammar or spelling, and they'll raise their little hands and put on that interested expression and ask you what games you played as a kid or who do you like for the goddam World Series. Oh, yeah. And you'll fall for it. Next thing is you're spilling your guts and they go home not knowing one end of a sentence from the other, but telling the moms and dads about your life. Not that they care. They'll get by, but where does that leave you? You can never get back the bits and pieces of your life that stick in their little heads. Your life, man. It's all you have. Tell 'em nothing.
The advice was wasted. I learned through trial and error and paid a price for it. I had to find my own way of being a man and a teacher and that is what I struggled with for thirty years in and out of the classrooms of New York. My students didn't know there was a man up there escaping a cocoon of Irish history and Catholicism, leaving bits of that cocoon everywhere.
My life saved my life. On my second day at McKee a boy asks a question that sends me into the past and colors the way I teach for the next thirty years. I am nudged into the past, the materials of my life.
Jo Santos calls out, Yo, teach...
You are not to call out. You are to raise your hand.

Yeah, yeah, said Joey, but ...
They have a way of saying yeah yeah that tells you they're barely tolerating you. In the yeah yeah they're saying, We're trying to be patient, man, giving you a break because you're just a new teacher.
Joey raised his hand. Yo, teacher man....
Call me Mr. McCourt.
Yeah. OK. So, you Scotch or somethin'?
Joey is the mouth. There's one in every class along with the complainer, the clown, the goody-goody, the beauty queen, the volunteer for everything, the jock, the intellectual, the momma's boy, the mystic, the sissy, the lover, the critic, the jerk, the religious fanatic who sees sin everywhere, the brooding one who sits in the back staring at the desk, the happy one, the saint who finds good in all creatures. It's the job of the mouth to ask questions, anything to keep the teacher from the boring lesson. I may be a new teacher but I'm on to Joey's delaying game. It's universal. I played the same game in Ireland. I was the mouth in my class in Leamy's National School. The master would write an algebra question or an Irish conjugation on the board and the boys would hiss, Ask him a question, McCourt. Get him away from the bloody lesson. Go on, go on.

A discussion of the task posed above may yield some of the following results:

Language development:	Learning new words like *jock* (so. who does lots of sport and is considered to be stupid)
Intercultural learning:	Realizing that playing the delaying game is a universal topic
Personal enrichment:	Comparing oneself with various learner roles (*complainer, clown, jerk*)
Motivational value:	Familiar setting (school), making sense of narrator's experiences
Interpretational openness:	Interpreting teacher roles (*collaborator, tap dancer, politician*), discussing veterans' advice
Social prestige:	Literature: high value, McCourt: Pulitzer Prize winner

2.2 Levels

At what age or level should teaching literature start?

Literature for all ages

Some people believe that literary texts cannot be integrated into the classroom until students have reached a level that is advanced enough for them to understand linguistic subtleties and grasp the full meaning. Such an attitude seems restricted and one-sided if we take a broad view of literature and believe that understanding and appreciating literature has to be gradually developed in a long process. Literature can be made use of at all levels – from beginners (6-11-year-olds depending on country and school system) to pre-intermediate and intermediate pupils (12-16 years) and finally advanced students (16+). The age and level of a group has to be considered, however, in terms of reading material, teaching goals and classroom procedures.

Literature for beginners

Beginners in the primary classroom enjoy short and funny texts such as rhymes, songs, stories or picture books. The methods and techniques used must take into account the developmental stage of the learners by resorting to playful learning, which appeals to many senses and is accompanied by movement, music as well as listening to and telling stories. The aim cannot be a critical analysis of texts but providing a first contact with literature, which promotes basic language skills, is fun and enhances the motivation to learn English.

Intermediate classes

Pre-intermediate and intermediate learners can cope with longer and linguistically more demanding texts. While or after working with the coursebook (which also contains short literary texts), teachers can add a *Begleitlektüre*, which has been written by the authors of the coursebook and is adapted to its lexis and grammar, or go for an *Anschlusslektüre*, which is independent of the coursebook and opens up more options. There are *graded readers*, which are specifically written for a certain language level (scope of words and grammatical structures), and *simplified readers*, which are shorter and linguistically less demanding adaptations of original novels or plays. Most schoolbook publishers now have a great number of titles, which enable teachers to practise different reading techniques and improve their students' understanding of literature, including global and detailed comprehension.

Advanced students

A full understanding and profound analysis of a literary text is usually reserved for advanced levels. At this stage, unabridged original works can be added – with or without annotations (explanations of words and cultural information). All reading techniques can be trained, creative writing and other forms of creating may become more sophisticated.

2.3 Places

Where can you teach and learn literature?

Classroom

The most obvious – but not the only – place for teaching literature is the *classroom*. Reading a book usually takes place at the same desk and on the same chair which are used for all the other classwork. If you are eager to instill in your students an awareness of the value of reading, your classroom should provide an environment in which reading is clearly cherished.

Reading corner

So a reading-ready classroom could contain a *reading corner*. In such a quiet and comfortable place, students can read independently or with a partner or small group. This reading area should include comfortable seating, for example bean bag chairs, pillows, carpet squares or even a small couch, a few plants and, for atmosphere, a couple of lamps. There are even some teachers who go for rather unconventional reading areas, putting up a tent, desgning a milk-jug igloo, or developing a reading garden – with a green carpet, a few lawn chairs, several plants and a piece of white lattice.

Classroom library

If you want to encourage independent reading, a *classroom library* is a must. It is advisable to set up your library in an area of the classroom which your students frequently pass by during the day. The classroom collection, which is usually stored in a bookcase with a display area, need not only consist of fictional materials but may offer a number of non-fiction and reference books. You should provide a wide range of genres, include a variety of topics, and look for titles which reflect student interests. Such a collection, presented in appropriate conditions, can create an atmosphere which is conducive to reading. So do not hide your books in closed shelves, but display as many of them as possible with covers visible at students' eye level. One of the weaknesses of a classroom library, of course, is that its collection is limited. If you are on a tight budget, you may set your hopes on the generosity of parents and friends or check out libraries (regular sales of used books), bargain areas of large bookstores, used book stores, flea sales, WWW auction sites, *remainder* sites carrying publishers' overstocks (www.bookcloseouts.com).

School library

Even if there is no classroom library, a *central library*, which constitutes an inclusive resource centre and serves all grades and subjects, is housed in most schools. It is inside the school premises, but outside the classroom, which is the problem. Students are not confronted with the store of books on a regular basis and so often forget about its existence. Therefore teachers should walk their students round the library and draw their attention to the supply of foreign language titles.

Home study

Reading literature can also be done *at home*, in one's study or favourite place in the house. Readers are free to choose when, where and how long to read. Moreover reading assignments for private study are many teachers' favourite pet as they save time for classroom discussion.

Public places

Learning from literature may not only take place at school or at home, but also in *public places*. Local libraries have English language titles as well as big bookstores, which provide similar sections and sometimes even a reading chair. In addition, there are several beyond-the-classroom programmes, which focus on encouraging reading in nonacademic settings. These innovative programmes take place in camps, libraries, clinics, and after-school settings – and in some cases it might be a good idea for a school teacher to cooperate with these institutions.

Internet reading

With the advent of the World Wide Web, *Internet reading* has become an alternative to print-based literature classes. Access to a web browser guarantees the availability of round-the-clock literature sources, and as more and more websites offer full-text options, reading a whole novel is just a mouse click away. Furthermore the hypertext structure allows a non-linear way of jumping across pages, and background study is supported by additional online material. However, this new medium is suitable for reading for information rather than reading for enjoyment. Scrolling down the pages, with your exes fixed on a small screen for hours, makes it hard to get lost in the world of a book – to be with it.

Mobile reading

The permanent availability of Internet literature also makes us aware that *mobile reading* is a modern-day option. Wireless LAN opens up immediate access to online texts, a short story may be stored on the notebook and read on the bus, audio fiction can be listened to via discman in the park, and a whole novel may even be read on one's private mobile phone.

In and out of the classroom

This short survey of venues makes clear that teaching literature is not confined to the classroom. Reading outside the formal classroom setting definitely helps children discover the pleasure of reading. However, to pass on the philosophy that reading is of high value it must not be compeletely 'outsourced' to places beyond the classroom, but has to remain an integral part of classroom time.

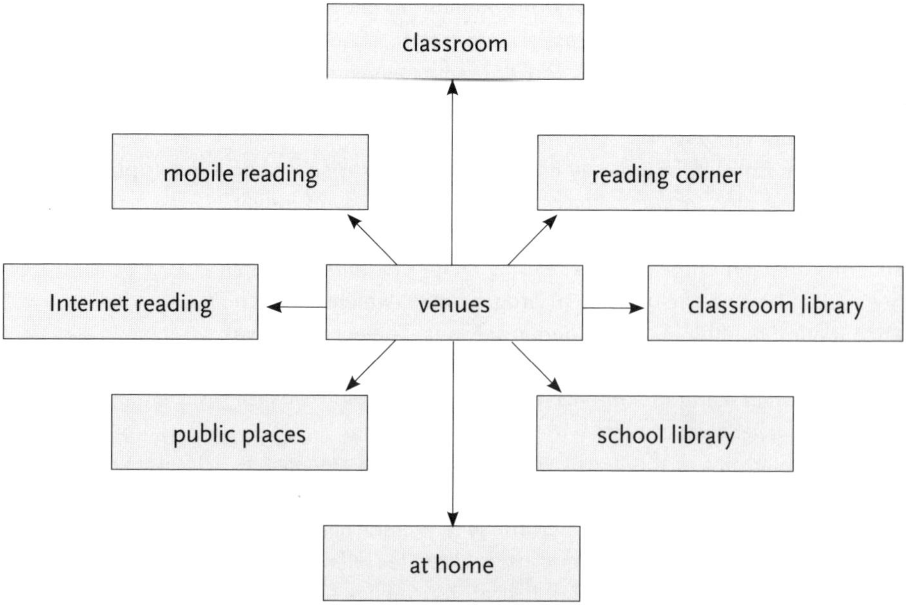

2.4 Objectives

What should students in our literature classes aim to achieve?

In the 1970s, Communicative Language Teaching (CLT) emerged as the dominant approach to teaching and learning a foreign language – if not at classroom level, then at least in academic discourse. CLT stresses the interactive nature of communication, i.e. people cooperate to negotiate meaning when communicating with each other, and it aims at *communicative competence* (CC). This goal comprises four competences: grammatical, discourse, sociocultural and strategic competence (Savignon 2001: 17). The first refers to phonological, lexical, morphological and syntactical language features on the sentence level; the second concerns the ability to form a meaningful oral and written text; the third deals with the social rules and culturally loaded meanings of language (politeness, turn-taking, appropriate content etc.), the fourth reminds us of the necessity of coping strategies (e.g. paraphrasing when you do not know a word). CC

In the field of intercultural learning, Michael Byram's model of Intercultural Communicative Competence (ICC, 1997) has gained much prominence. ICC here comprises skills, knowledge, attitudes and education and consists of five competences or *savoirs*: skills of interpreting and relating (*savoir comprendre*), skills of discovering and/or interacting (*savoir apprendre/faire*), knowledge of self and other (*savoirs*), attitudes of relativising self and valuing other (*savoir être*), and political education/critical cultural awareness (*savoir s'engager*). ICC

Drawing on those two models, i.e. CLT and ICC, the goal when teaching and learning literature in class may be found in LCC: Literary Communicative Competence. Such a target also comprises knowledge, attitudes and various skills, i.e. reading, understanding (analysing, interpreting), and creating. The three domains of knowledge, skills and attitudes as well as the three skills just mentioned must be seen against the background of communication. They should not be dealt with as separate dimensions, but foster literature-based communication and negotiation of meaning. LCC

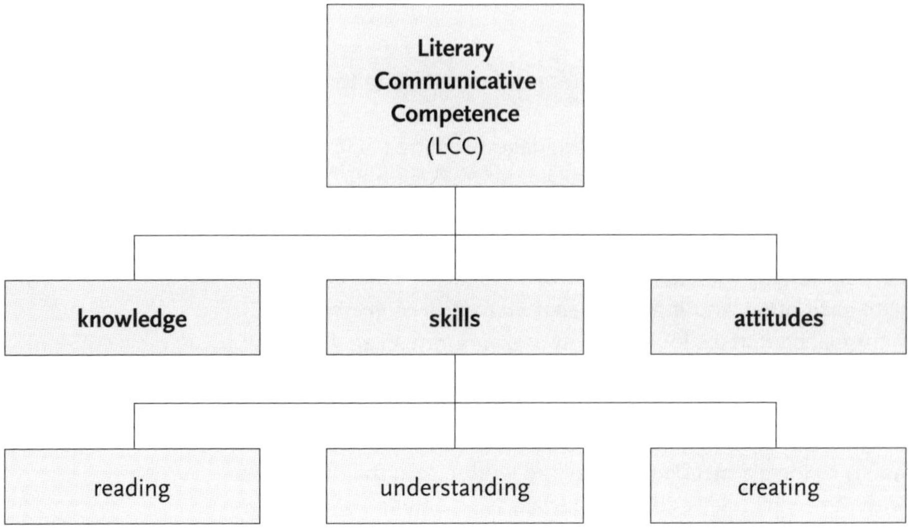

Tasks

1. Choose one play or novel, and check whether it is suitable for an advanced class by applying the various criteria of selection.
2. Show that one piece of literature, e.g. R.L. Stevenson's novel *Treasure Island*, can be used at all levels – for beginners, intermediate and advanced students.
3. Research what literature in digital form can be studied via the Gutenberg project: www.gutenberg.com.
4. Re-read the excerpt from Frank McCourt's *Teacher Man* and illustrate how the four dimensions of *communicative competence* – according to Savignon – can be encouraged by giving one example each.

Goals

3 Knowledge

3.1 Literary history

Is it really necessary to know when a piece of literature was written?

Relevance of literary history

Having an overview of literary history can be helpful in several ways. A general knowledge of the main periods of history helps to orientate the readers and eases their understanding of the details of a specific work. You also avoid the potential danger of misreading a text through ignorance of its historical setting. Finally, the broader your information about the period in which a text was written, the more appealing and fascinating it will become to you personally. Your experience of literature will be enriched if you know about the prevailing attitudes of the period towards the individual, society, the state, education, money, duty, ethics, art, and love.

Qualifications to the period concept

The following table lists dates, periods and some outstanding authors of each period of British and Irish literature (also see Nünning/Nünning 2004: 162ff.). Students should be made aware of several qualifications to the period concept, which is a literary construct rather than a real object. Firstly, the periods or movements are rather general terms, which may be subdivided further. Then the characteristics that mark certain periods are always relative, as works written in one era often show similarities with works of other periods, and no individual work can ever embody all the features associated with a given period. Moreover the beginning and the end of each era cannot be fixed precisely, boundaries are permeable as the periods overlap and have various transitional phases; and terminal dates vary from one country to another. The labeling of literary periods does not always appear to be consistent either because the traditional names derive from a variety of sources, e.g. 'Renaissance' comes from art history, 'Restoration' from political history, 'The Eighteenth Century' is chronological, 'Romantic' is from literary theory, while 'Elizabethan' and 'Victorian' refer to the names of reigning monarchs. Finally, the list of authors should not be misinterpreted as a canon but rather a selective choice of some highly acclaimed writers.

History of English literature

Periods	*Characteristics*	*Authors (Works)*
Old English (Anglo-Saxon) period (450 – 1066)	From oral tradition to written literature, biblical and religious themes	Caedmon, Cynewulf, *Beowulf* (great Germanic epic poem)
Middle English period (1066 – 1500)	Religious and secular writings, *Mystery Plays, Morality Plays*	Geoffrey Chaucer: *The Canterbury Tales*; Anon.: *Sir Gawain and the Green Knight*
Renaissance (1500 – 1660)	Poetry, prose and drama, 4 subsets: Elizabethan Age (1558-1603), Jacobean Age (1603-1625), Caroline Age (1625-1649), Commonwealth Period (or Puritan Interregnum) (1649-1660)	John Donne, Ben Jonson, Christopher Marlowe, Andrew Marvell, Thomas Morus, William Shakespeare
Restoration (1660 – 1700)	Restoration of monarchy, reason and tolerance, comedy of manners *(Restoration Comedy)*	Samuel Butler, William Congreve, John Dryden, John Milton, William Wycherley
Augustan Age (1700 – 1745)	neoclassicism (Roman emperor Augustus: Vergil, Ovid), refinement and elegance, *Age of Pope*, first English novels	Daniel Defoe, Alexander Pope, Samuel Richardson, Jonathan Swift
Age of Sensibility (1745 – 1785)	*Age of Johnson*, enlightenment, instinct and feeling, fine novels	Henry Fielding, Samuel Johnson, Laurence Sterne
Romantic period (1785 – 1830)	personal nature, power of feeling, symbolism, focus on nature and the supernatural, *Gothic literature* (dark settings, fantastic plots)	Jane Austen, William Blake, George Byron, Samuel Coleridge, Walter Scott, Percy Shelley, Mary Shelley, William Wordsworth
Victorian era (1837 – 1901)	reign of Queen Victoria, social, economic, religious and political issues of the day, *Pre-Raphaelites, Aestheticism and Decadence*	Brontë sisters, Charles Dickens, D. G. Rossetti, R. L. Stevenson, Alfred Tennyson, W. M. Thackeray, Oscar Wilde

Edwardian era (1901 – 1914)	King Edward VII, height of British Empire, class-ridden society, social problems of the majority	Joseph Conrad, E.M. Forster, John Galsworty, Thomas Hardy, G.B. Shaw, H.G. Wells, W. B. Yeats
Modernism (1914 – 1945)	Experimenting with form, style, subject matter	W.H. Auden, T.S. Eliot, James Joyce, D.H. Lawrence, J.B. Priestley, Dylan Thomas, Virginia Woolf
Post-war era (Postmodern period) (1945 – 2007)	Blending literary genres and styles, breaking free from modernist forms	Julian Barnes, Samuel Beckett, Caryl Churchill, Seamus Heaney, Ted Hughes, Kazuo Ishiguro, David Lodge, Ian McEwan, John Osborne, Harold Pinter, Peter Shaffer, Tom Stoppard

American literary history

The periodization of American literature is done in a similar way. Due to a lack of ruling dynasties, other criteria, however, are employed such as aesthetic topoi, political events and socio-cultural trends. The following table again gives a simplified and selective overview of American literary history (also see Nünning/Nünning 2004: 165, Zapf 1997, Wagner 2003).

American literary history

Periods	*Characteristics*	*Authors*
Colonial period (1607 – mid-18th century)	Practical, religious, or historical themes	Anne Bradstreet, John Winthrop, Benjamin Franklin
Literature of the early republic (mid-18th – early 19th century)	Beginnings of truly *American* literature (authentic settings, themes, characters)	*Connecticut Wits*, James Cooper, Washington Irving
Romantic period – American Renaissance, Age of Transcendentalism (1830 – 1860)	Original pieces shaping the ideas and ideals of many American writers	Emily Dickinson, R. W. Emerson, Nathaniel Hawthorne, H. W. Longfellow, Herman Melville, E. A. Poe, H. B. Stowe, Walt Whitman
Realism (1865 – 1900)	*Realistic* fiction, representing life as it really is, focusing on the ordinary and commonplace	Kate Chopin, Bret Harte, Henry James, Mark Twain, Edith Wharton

Naturalism (1900 – 1914)	Trying to give an even more accurate depiction of life than realism, presenting subjects with a scientific objectivity	Stephen Crane, Theodore Dreiser, Jack London, Frank Norris
Modernism (1910 – 1945)	Experimenting with subject matter, form, and style - Jazz Age - Harlem Renaissance - The Lost Generation	E.E. Cummings, William Faulkner, F. S. Fitzgerald, Robert Frost, Ernest Hemingway, Langston Hughes, Arthur Miller, Eugene O'Neill, K. A. Porter, Ezra Pound, Gertrude Stein, Thornton Wilder, Tennessee Williams
Contemporary – post-modernism to present day (1939 – 2007)	To be decided (tbd): various trends, time will tell	Edward Albee, Paul Auster, Saul Bellow, Charles Bukowski, Truman Capote, Louise Erdrich, Jonathan Franzen, Toni Morrison, Vladimir Nabokov, J. C. Oates, Sylvia Plath, Philip Roth, Sam Shepard, John Updike

3.2 Literary theory

What approaches to literary criticism do you know?

Literary theory and literary criticism

Whereas literary history is primarily concerned with historical areas of inquiry, literary theory deals with the systematic areas of literary studies (Murray 1999, Habib 2005, Nünning/Nünning 2004). Some scholars make a distinction between literary criticism, which focuses on the study, discussion, evaluation, and interpretation of literary texts, and literary theory, which probes the fundamental questions of literature (nature, goals, methods). Literary criticism then often becomes a practical application of theory, as it deals directly with a piece of literature. Many scholars, however, make no distinction between the two terms and use them together to describe the same concept.

Research domains

Literary theory covers many areas of research. It deals with the definition of literature, theories of interpretation, classifications

Hostility to theory usually means an opposition to other people's theories and an oblivion of one's own.
Terry Eagleton

of works, genre theory, literary aesthetics (beauty, taste), and poetics (literary art). Textual criticism, i.e. assessing whether a textual edition is reliable, and scholarly editing, i.e. providing critical editions of major works, may also be included.

Relevance of literary theory

A certain acquaintance with the most important issues of literary theory is a necessity for teachers and students alike. If learners claim they do not need theoretical background but want a 'direct', 'unbiased' approach to a text, they are not aware of their hidden theoretical and methodological premises. An insight into literary theory helps them to discover their own subconscious guidelines of judgement. Moreover they will understand secondary literature only if they have a basic knowledge of relevant categories. Equipped with a certain awareness of literary theory, they can also choose those approaches and models which are most suited to the text they are studying. So literary theory and literary criticism "are indispensable analytical tools, which enable the student to formulate the premises and arguments of their literary analyses, to describe textual phenomena in an appropriately differentiated manner, and to render their analytical approaches transparent and their interpretative conclusions comprehensible" (Nünning/Nünning 1998: 35).

Approaches to literary theory

Teachers and, to a certain degree, students should therefore have a preliminary overview of the most important theories, models and approaches. Nünning/Nünning distinguish between text-oriented, author-oriented, reader-oriented, and context-oriented approaches (1998: 38ff.). The following table gives a very brief survey of some major schools of literary theory together with some of their representatives – a reduction in the complexity of these approaches is inevitable in such a description.

Major approaches to literary theory

Term	*Representatives*	*Approach*
Formalism	Roman Jakobson, René Wellek, Austin Warren	Viewing literary language as self-focused; studying the language of a literary text; focusing on the 'formal' features of language

Hermeneutics	H. G. Gadamer, Erich Auerbach, E.D. Hirsch	Seeing interpretation as a circular process (*hermeneutischer Zirkel*); interplay between our sense of the whole and our understanding of its component parts; importance of interpreter
New Criticism	I.A. Richards, W.K. Wimsatt, F.R. Leavis	Treating a work as autonomous; looking at it on the basis of what is written (*close reading*), not at the author's intention or biography or its relationship to literary history
New Historicism	Stephen Greenblatt, Louis Montrose, Michel Foucault	Being against the 'ahistorical' approach of New Criticism; examining a text by also studying other texts of the same time period; viewing history broadly and sceptically
Structuralism	Roman Jakobson, Claude Lévi-Strauss, Roland Barthes	Concerned with the description of structure; regarding any element as determined by all the other elements in a situation; examining the underlying structures in the content of a text
Reception / Reader Response Theory	Louise Rosenblatt, Wolfgang Iser, Stanley Fish	Seeing reading as a dialectical process between reader and text; focusing upon the active response of the reader to a text; dependent on a reader's 'interpretive community'
Post-structuralism, Deconstructivism	Michel Foucault, Roland Barthes, Jacques Derrida	Against seeing language as a closed system; viewing literature as irreducibly plural and an endless play of signifiers; negating a single meaning; accepting shifting meanings; interpretation is constantly self-conscious

(Neo-) Marxism	Karl Marx, Georg Lukacs, Theodor Adorno	Viewing literary works as the products of historical forces; looking at the material conditions of the age; emphasizing themes of class conflict (dominant vs. repressed classes), exploitation, alienation, *Sein – Bewusstsein*
Psychoanalytical Approach	Sigmund Freud, Jacques Lacan, Shoshona Felman	Applying (Freud's, Lacan's) psychological principles to the study of literature; focusing on the author's psyche, the effects of literature upon the readers, the creative process, psychological principles within works of literature
Feminism	Luce Irigaray, Judith Butler, Elaine Showalter	Discussing the role of gender identity/relations in literature; establishing a feminist canon; interpreting from a less patriarchal slant
Postcolonialism	Chinua Achebe, Wole Soyinka, Salman Rushdie	Examining the culture (e.g. literature) of former colonies of the European empires, and their relation to the rest of the world; studying imperialism, Eurocentrism, hybridity, or alterity (otherness)

An example

Suppose a novel started with the simple sentence: "There was an apple on the table." The different schools of literary theory would ask different questions.

Formalism:	What is the size and shape of this apple?
Hermeneutics:	What is the relation between the apple and the rest of the table?
New Criticism:	What do the words "There was ... table" mean?
New Historicism:	How many people buy apples in this age?

Structuralism:	How is the skin related to the other elements of the apple?
Reader Response:	How does the apple smell and taste to me?
Marxism:	Who is the owner of the apple?
Deconstructivism:	If the skin and the flesh are both part of the apple, are they not in fact one and the same thing?
Psychoanalysis:	What does the apple remind us of?
Feminism:	What chances are there for a woman who eats this apple?
Postcolonialism:	Who does not own this apple?

Methodological pluralism

So knowing about different approaches helps us to ask more questions. It is not advisable to look with an uncritical eye at only one approach. An open-minded attitude towards a methodological pluralism makes it easier for us to choose the appropriate approach. This choice depends on the particular text given, its genre and time of publication, as well as the task and the objective of our interpretation.

Intertextuality and intermediality

We should, however, not only see a text as a single entity, but be aware of intertextuality and intermediality. An intertextual approach discloses similarities between different texts and systematically investigates the relationships between texts and genres. The rise of modern media has also necessitated intermedial approaches, which examine the interplay between different types of texts and media (e.g. book and film, song, music video).

Literary terminology

Apart from studying the macro level of literary theories, models and approaches, we must also know the tools on the micro level of classroom analysis. There are numerous rhetorical devices from A for assonance to Z for zeugma, the meanings of which teachers and students have to learn. The most important literary terms will be dealt with in the following chapters.

Tasks

1. Let's play *Who Wants To Be A Millionaire?* The following questions (€ 50 – € 1,000,000) were actually asked in the German TV version hosted by Günther Jauch. Now try to reach the million.

€ 50,–

Captain Ahab is chasing ...

A. Kimba, the white lion

B. Doctor Kimble

C. Herman Melville

D. Moby Dick

€ 100,–

What is the typical opening formula of fairy tales?

A. Well, yes, you know ...

B. Once upon a time ...

C. And they lived happily hereafter.

D. Na gut, ich sach mal ...

€ 200,–

Who invented the detectives Miss Marple and Hercule Poirot?

A. Mark Twain

B. Raymond Chandler

C. Dashiell Hammett

D. Agatha Christie

€ 300,–

What is one comedy by Shakespeare called?

A. As You Like It

B. As You Want to Come

C. As The Beak Grows

D. What, This Does Not Work?

€ 500,–

Who wrote *St. Clare's* (Hanni und Nanni) and *The Famous Five (Die fünf Freunde)*?

A. Enid Blyton
B. Jo Pestum
C. Karl May
D. Astrid Lindgren

€ 1,000,–

What was James Joyce?

A. Scottish rebel
B. Western hero
C. author
D. deep sea diver

€ 2,000,–

Which absurd drama made Irishman Samuel Beckett world famous?

A. Waiting for Easter
B. Waiting for Godot
C. Waiting for the bus
D. Waiting for Vladimir

€ 4,000,–

How did Ernest Hemingway die?

A. murder
B. suicide
C. car accident
D. old age

€ 8,000,–
What is a *haiku*?

A. thatched cottage | B. poem
C. sauna stove | D. sword

€ 16,000,–
Who wrote the trilogy of novels *Lord of the Rings*?

A. Ende | B. Verne
C. Tolkien | D. Greene

€ 32,000,–
Who wrote the novel *The Great Gatsby*?

A. Francis Scott Fitzgerald | B. Ernest Hemingway
C. Arthur Conan Doyle | D. Charles Dickens

€ 64,000,–
Which of these persons really lived?

A. Cyrano de Bergerac | B. Sherlock Holmes
C. Tarzan | D. Count of Monte Christo

€ 125,000,–

What are the names of the feuding families Romeo and Juliet from Shakespeare's drama belong to?

A. Montague and Capulet | B. Escaron and Tybalt
C. Güldenstern and Mercutio | D. Desdemona and Turandot

€ 500,000,–

What is the name of Bret Easton Ellis' controversial novel made into a film starring Christian Bale?

A. American Psycho | B. Lolita
C. Story of O. | D. Lust

€ 1,000,000,–

Which pop band called itself after a character in a novel by Charles Dickens?

A. Jethro Tull | B. Uriah Heep
C. Boney M. | D. Fleetwood Mac

2. In the following, each approach to literary criticism is represented by three key items. Try to find out what these concepts mean by doing research using printed or digital sources.
- Hermeneutics: intentionality, *Dasein*, phenomenological reduction
- New Criticism: intentional fallacy, affective fallacy, close reading

- New Historicism: thick description, self-positioning, episteme
- Reception and Reader-Response Theory: implied reader, transactional analysis, horizons of expectations
- Structuralism: binary opposition, sign, narratology
- Feminism: patriarchy, androgyny, second-wave and third-wave feminism
- Psychoanalytical Approach: unconscious, Freud's model of the psyche, Lacan's model of the psyche
- Marxism: dialectical materialism, conspicuous consumption, superstructure
- Postcolonialism: hybridity, Eurocentrism, diaspora
- Deconstructivism: logocentrism, aporia, erasure

4 Skills

4.1 Reading

Are you a good reader? Why (not)?

Bottom-up model

As for the reading process, three theories may be distinguished. The *bottom-up* view (or *outside-in* view) of reading holds that reading is basically a matter of decoding a series of written symbols into their aural equivalents in the quest to make sense of the text (Grabe/Stoller 2002:31). Novice readers acquire a set of hierarchically ordered sub-skills that sequentially build toward comprehension ability. Meaning resides in the text on the printed page, and the reader has to reproduce meaning – going from letter to syllable to word to phrase to clause to sentence to paragraph to text. This traditional model of reading has often been under attack as it relies on the formal features of the language, mainly words and structure. It must be admitted, however, that knowledge of linguistic features is also necessary to understand a text.

Top-down model

To counteract over-reliance on structure, the *top-down view* (or *cognitive view*) was introduced. Here, the reader rather than the text is at the heart of the reading process. Reading is seen as a psycholinguistic guessing game, in which readers sample the text, make hypotheses, confirm or reject them, make new hypotheses, and so on. In this process, the readers make use of their background knowledge (world knowledge, topic knowledge) and so-called schemata, i.e. "building blocks of cognition" which are used when interpreting sensory data, retrieving information from memory, organising goals and subgoals. If our schemata are incomplete and do not provide an understanding of the incoming data from the text we will face problems understanding the text. In the top-down model the constructive nature of comprehension is emphasized, form and structure, however, are neglected.

Interactive model

The bottom-up, language-based and the top-down, knowledge-based perspectives are integrated in the *interactive view* (or *metacognitive view*). "The 'construction' of meaning that occurs in reading is a combination of 'bottom-up' processes [decoding and understanding words, phrases and sentences in the text] and 'top-down ones [our expectations, previous knowledge constructs (schemata) of the text content and genre] ... Thus learners should be encouraged to combine top-down and bottom-up strategies in reading" (Ur 1996:141).

bottom-up model	focus on text	• from part to whole • from letters to words to paragraphs to sentences to text
top-down model	focus on reader	• from whole to part • reader: expectations, schemata • background knowledge (world knowledge, topic knowledge), inferencing
interactive model	focus on integration	combination of bottom-up and top-down processes

Supporting the interactive process

Reading instruction can encourage an interactive approach, i.e. a synthesis of bottom-up and top-down processes, in various ways. Language awareness including an awareness of phonemes and the ability to process words automatically and rapidly has to be developed. Before the actual act of reading a text begins, some points should be looked at in order to aid understanding. In pre-reading activities it is important to provide the necessary background information to the reader to facilitate understanding. The reader's existing knowledge before reading the text is drawn on so that background knowledge can be linked to new information more easily and thoroughly. The texts chosen should contain words and grammatical structures familiar to the learners, and teachers can introduce unknown key vocabulary, main ideas and the conceptual framework beforehand. The topics of the texts should be in accordance with the age range, gender, interests, and background culture of the students for whom they are intended. It is also necessary for students to become aware of the purpose for reading, for example the students may be guided to ask themselves: "What do I want to know after reading this passage?" Students must also learn to recognize the type of text before reading, as texts take on different forms and hold certain pieces of information in different places. If they understand the layout of the material being read they can focus more deeply on the parts that are more densely packed with information. Paying attention to the year a certain text was published may help the reader to anticipate and predict the actual content as can looking at the name of the author and the rest of the reference apparatus (blurb, biographical information, table of contents, foreword, preface, illustrations etc.). Finally students must be able to choose an appropriate reading style (scanning, skimming etc.).

Reading styles	
skimming (reading for gist)	scanning (reading for specific information)
intensive reading (reading for detailed understanding)	extensive reading (reading for global understanding)
reading aloud	silent reading
reading for information	reading for pleasure
critical reading (context, purpose, ideology)	naïve reading

A Bluffer's Guide

The following book report is written in the style of a bluffer's guide, i.e. a tongue-in-cheek advice on how to sound informed and cheat in literature exams. It is accompanied by a number of tasks to illustrate different reading styles.

The Bluffer's Guide to The Catcher in the Rye

Synopsis

16-year-old Holden Caulfield is in a crisis. He skips school and wanders through New York for three days. ... Afterwards he checks into a sanatorium.

Possible interpretation

The Catcher is the novel of puberty. The main protagonist is having problems adjusting to the educational system. He seeks the kind of beauty and higher truth that isn't taught at school.

So what's it really about?
16-year-old guy cleverly manages to win over girls' hearts by coming across all sensitive.

Do say:
"Holden is a character both too simple and too complex to fully comprehend. The novel avoids a final judgement, so that the reader is left to decide for himself. One thing's for sure, though: It's a work of great importance."

Don't say:
"Who's catching? Is Hulk Hogan in it?"

Example: reading tasks

Possible reading tasks may include:
- Skimming: What is this guide about?
- Scanning: What is said about the ...?
- Intensive reading: Analyse the interpretation.
- Reading aloud: Read out the synopsis.
- Did you read this guide for information or for pleasure?
- Critical reading: Is it right to produce such bluffer's guides?

Pros and cons of reading styles

Each reading style has its benefits and drawbacks. The following survey attempts a summary of the pros and cons of four important styles.

Style	**Benefits**	**Drawbacks**
Reading aloud	• Practising pronunciation • Same reading speed for all • For younger learners	• Slow and uniform pace • Focus on phonological surface • Distracting from deep semantic understanding
Silent reading	• Natural way of reading • Fast and individual pace • Focus on understanding	• Different speeds in class • No pronunciation practice
Intensive reading	• Detailed understanding • Focus on accuracy	• Tedious over-analysis • Time-consuming
Extensive reading	• Reading much, fast, individually • Reading for pleasure/fun reading • Focus on fluency	• Lack of detailed understanding • Lack of control

The active reader

Metacognition involves thinking about what one is doing during the reading. Therefore while-reading activities must be integrated to make use of the reader's resources during text processing and encourage active reading. Such strategic readers summarize, question, evaluate, and place a text within their own experience. They try to locate a topic sentence and follow supporting details toward a conclusion, make continuous predictions about what will occur next, establish whole-part relationships, compare and contrast, determine cause-effect, infer, and conclude. These processes may be very difficult to develop in a classroom setting, yet students must be encouraged to enter into a dialogue with what they are reading. In this process, *the 10 commandments for the active reader* may be a humorous reminder.

The 10 commandments for the active reader

1. *Thou shalt read a lot.*
2. *Thou shalt predict what is going to happen next in the text in order to combine what has come before with what will happen after.*
3. *Thou shalt use your prior knowledge by activating background information and schemata.*
4. *Thou shalt read as fast as possible by getting used to reading in chunks (groups of words), but also vary your reading speed according to purpose.*
5. *Thou shalt love reading.*
6. *Thou shalt have a clear purpose for reading.*
7. *Thou shalt use different reading strategies for different kinds of reading.*
8. *Thou shalt concentrate on the important points and skip insignificant pieces.*
9. *Thou shalt pause at certain places while reading a text to absorb the material being read and sort out information.*
10. *Thou need not understand every single unknown word but should guess its meaning from context, word family, or other languages.*

Post-reading stage

Although while- and after-reading activities sometimes overlap, it seems justified to posit a post-reading stage. The activities in this third phase depend on the purpose of reading and the type of information extracted from the text. In general, they revolve around (detailed) comprehension, (close) analysis, (creative) production, and (media-oriented) transformation. So teachers may resort to discussing the text in written or oral form, summarizing, posing or answering questions, completing texts, filling in forms as well as writing reading logs, role-playing, creating radio plays, or reading other related materials.

PWP approach

As there are three stages of reading a text, a lesson may be structured along them. The following table summarizes the three stages of the *pwp approach*, including a few ideas for the pre-reading, while-reading, and post-reading stages (also see Hinz 1996).

Pre-reading stage	• predicting from title, cover, chapter headings, pictures • information on author, date of publication • introduction to plot, topic, main characters, key words • brainstorming, heartstorming, opinion poll • upside down comprehension • writing a short text (on key word, key passage, first sentence) • provocative statement, vote a quote, pyramid discussion • visual media • acoustic impulse
While-reading stage	• listening (CD, teacher's voice) • checking against predictions, guiding questions • completing charts, grids, flow charts, profiles • visualizing, drawing • stopping at key points and reflecting • BUT: don't put the learner off reading ▶ don't overdo while-reading tasks
Post-reading stage	• detailed comprehension • close analysis • text production • imagining, changing • visual, auditory, scenic transformation

The virtuous circle

A clear structure of a reading unit along with a well chosen text and motivating tasks may help to set the *virtuous circle of the good reader* in action – and stop the *vicious cycle of the bad reader* (Nuttall 1987).

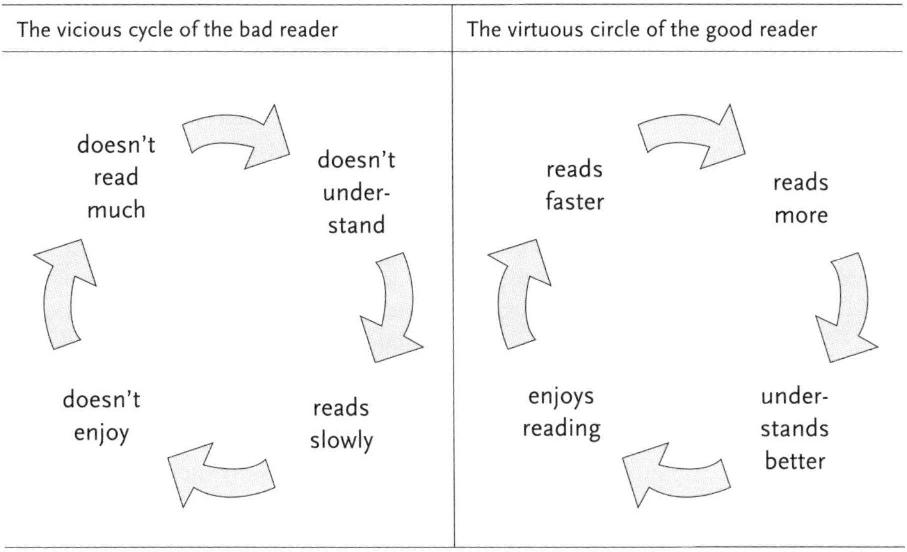

4.2 Understanding

How can you achieve an understanding of a literary text?

Analysis – interpretation – understanding

Reading a text is not synonymous with understanding it. If you examine it more closely, you may reach a deeper appreciation of it in the end. To describe this process, various terms are employed, the most common being *analysis* and *interpretation*. The former usually means studying the individual components of a text, the latter tries to explore the potential meanings of it. The term *understanding* is employed here to cover both perspectives.

Hermeneutics

The process of understanding, i.e. explaining, analysing, interpreting a text, is often called *hermeneutics* (3.2). An important element of this approach is the so-called *hermeneutic circle*, which refers to the notion that your understanding of a text as a whole is established by reference to the individual parts, and your understanding of each individual part by reference to the whole. It is a circle as neither the whole text nor any individual part of it can be understood without reference to each other.

Modern approaches to literary theory like Reception Theory, Reader Response Theory or Deconstructivism, however, have made clear that there is not a single meaning to a text, but a variety of possible meanings dependent on variables like the reader, the social situation or historical period of interpretation. Within the context of the language classroom, this means saying farewell to the existence of a single interpretation dictated by the teacher or some printed model solution. It is the learner-centred process of attributing meaning to a text rather than the product which counts in language lessons.

Criteria of analysis

Learner-centredness – and learning-centredness – should not be mistaken for arbitrariness. The famous *anything goes* does not mean that any interpretation is valid (on the contrary postmodernist analysis is self-conscious and constantly on guard), but students must justify their conclusions and check them against the text. A valuable analysis and interpretation must observe certain criteria such as clarity, precision, comprehensibility, coherence, systematic application of analytical categories, reference to secondary literature (Nünning/Nünning 2004: 24 f.).

Pragmatic view

Although these and other criteria may be helpful guidelines, we should not expect them to lead our students to a full understanding of literature. From a pragmatic point of view, their literary background and their foreign language competence are not elaborate enough to enable an interpretation which satisfies our literary scholars. It is not possible to cover all literary categories, and to probe too deep into any one of them. They first have to understand the basic principles of signification and discourse (meanings of a sentence, syntax, cohesion, coherence etc.). Then they may examine a few aspects of both theme (content) and form (composition) of a text, i.e. the *what* and *how* of it. Such an investigation should not only identify certain thematic and formal characteristics, but also discuss their *functions*, i.e. their effects within and beyond the text.

Global-to-detail approach

To support understanding in the classroom, a literature unit should have a clear structure (Thaler 2012). One approach is based on pre-, while-, and post-reading activities (4.1). A similar way of structuring a reading lesson is the *global-to-detail approach*, which proceeds from a global comprehension of the text to a more detailed one and may end in a deeper understanding. As it requires a double reading of the same text (passage), it is more suitable for shorter texts. The six steps are:

Global-to-detail approach	
Step	*Some Activities*
(1) Lead-in	• Introducing topic • Raising motivation • Giving background knowledge (author, period) • Introducing key vocabulary • Setting pre-tasks (e.g. predicting)
(2) First reading	• Skimming text / passage • Silent reading
(3) Global comprehension	• Questions • Answers to pre-tasks
(4) Second reading	• Intensive reading (aloud) • Scanning
(5) Detailed comprehension	• Questions • Explaining difficult words
(6) Understanding	• Examining rhetorical elements • Exploring potential meanings

4.3 Creating

How can you work creatively with a text?

Forms of creating

Apart from reading, analysing and interpreting a text, learners should also be allowed to relate to a text on a creative level. Individually, in pairs or small groups, they may present their personal perspectives on a text (Caspari 1994, Hinz 1996, Thaler 2011). This need not be restricted to the written mode, but can include spoken, visual, scenic, acoustic and manual forms.

Creating	
Medium	*Examples*
Written creations	• Creative writing (see below)
Spoken creations	• Filling in indeterminacies (*Leerstellen*) • Reciting in various moods, pitches, volumes

Scenic creations	• Role playing, acting • Miming, frozen tableau • *Hot seat* • Interviewing • Making a shadow play, puppet show
Visual creations	• Drawing pictures, designing collages • Making a comic • Drawing a structure chart (incl. key phrases) • Making a literature magazine
Acoustic creations	• Putting the text into sound • Reading with suitable background music
Manual creations	• Designing objects from the text • Cooking British food

Creative writing

The most popular of these modes of creation, however, still seems to be creative writing. Among the numerous definitions, the one by Holtwisch is particularly suitable for language classroom purposes; he regards those procedures as 'creative' "die Texte um-, nach- oder neu gestalten oder sie in andere Medien umsetzen" (Holtwisch 1999:417). Creative writing can serve a lot of linguistic, communicative, affective and social purposes: complementing teacher-centred textual analysis, expressing personal experiences, experimenting with a foreign language, discovering one's own personality, getting to know other persons, developing one's own planning and writing strategies, enlarging one's vocabulary, fostering self-determination and freedom of expression, raising motivation, and improving class atmosphere (Beyer-Kessling 2002:334; Holtwisch 1999:418). These positive effects, however, are dependent on certain conditions. The students' imagination must be activated by some stimuli, they must get informed about text types and text structures, and they must become aware of writing as a process.

Process view of creative writing

Bludau (1998:14) distinguishes between pre-writing, writing, and post-writing. Froese (1999:426f.) divides the process of creative writing into four phases: inspiration (collecting ideas), incubation (playful experimenting with material), illumination (writing), and verification (editing and publishing). Kieweg (2003) even offers six stages (idea, structure, writing strategies, first draft, editing, final text). All of these models emphasize how important it is for the teacher to draw students' attention to writing as a process. The first version of a text need not be perfect, but can be edited as to form, content, addressee, or spelling.

Stimuli for creative writing

Before students can start writing, they must get a stimulus and be put into the proper writing mood. Such a stimulus can take on various forms and trigger off different tasks, as the following table shows.

Stimulus	**Tasks**
Complete text	• Sentence switchboards • Transformation tasks (different genre) • Changing the narrative perspective • Changing persons, times, places
Incomplete text	• Completing open-ended stories • Writing the ending • Filling in missing parts • Enlarging a skeleton text
Missing text	• Writing on a title • About myself: I am ..., I like ..., ABCs • Anagrams, acrostics • Responding to a newspaper's problem page • Chain writing, taking turns
Text structure given	• Parodying a fairy tale • Creating advertisements, responding to an ad • Writing a love story • Designing a crossword puzzle (with the PC)
Acoustic stimulus	• Associations with noises • Listening to music: collecting words, writing a story
Visual stimulus	• Writing a story matching a photo/picture • Cartoon, collages, videos, realia, sculpture • Shape poems

Example of guided writing

The skill of creative writing has to be developed successively in a long process. Learners need help in the form of instructions, skeletons or schemes to gradually process their ideas. A nice example of skeleton writing, which guides the students step by step to more autonomous writing products and is based on collaborative work, is suggested by Harm (1997). The first step is to give them a "short science-fiction-horror short story" in the form of a framework with different options (boxes) on each level. By following the arrows, they select their own story until they reach a box with "The end". They write down their story and give it to another pupil, which allows some enjoyable reading. The second step is to give them another framework ("a crazy love story"), in which the boxes now are empty. Guided by general instructions (e.g. 'person', or 'place', or 'adjective'), they fill in the boxes. Then they exchange their story scheme with one by another pupil and write a story by drawing lines. The final step is for them to create their own framework for writing a short story on a topic like "Life in 2020".

Example: rewriting song lyrics

Another idea is to study the lyrics of a popular song and rewrite the text. An amusing example is the theme song for Wikipediholics, i.e. people who spend excessive time at the Wikipedia website. It should be sung to the tune of the Eagles classic *Hotel California*.

Hotel Wikipedia

On a dark office evening,
Sat down in my chair.
Sharp smell of stale coffee
Circling round in the air.

Suddenly on the webpage
There came a flickering light.
My head grew heavy, and my sight grew dim;
I had to stop for the night.

There it was in the link list:
"Edit page; you'll do well"
And I was thinking to myself
This could be Heaven or this could be Hell!

Then it lit up the quickbar
And it showed me the way.
There were pages begging for clean-up;
I thought I heard them say:

Welcome to the Hotel Wikipedia
Such a lovely place
So much empty space
Plenty of work at the Hotel Wikipedia
Any time of year
You can find us here...

source: Wikipedia, Wikipediholics Anonymous

Teaching Unit

Creative writing may also be integrated into longer teaching units. A project centred around fairy tales and covering 16 lessons is suggested by Tendel (2007) for intermediate classes. The students' creative texts are collected in nice folders (portfolios) and illustrated with drawings and photos.

Teaching Unit	
Topic:	Fairy and Fantasy Tales
Aims:	– reading fairy and fantasy tales – studying the genre of fairy tale – creative writing – telling stories
Level:	grade 8
Time:	8 double lessons
Procedure:	– 1st double lesson: *Jack and the Beanstalk* as gapped text, pupils fill in the gaps, read out and correct the different versions in small groups, final grammar focus on past tense – 2nd double lesson: *The Three Wishes*, first part of text presented in jumbled order, pupils reconstruct the text, study the characteristics of a fairy tale, write the ending of the tale – 3rd double lesson: pupils read and discuss the different endings, 40 coloured photos are put on the floor, each pupil chooses one, in groups of five they justify their choice, then they think of a story in which all five photos play a role, finally they present these stories – 4th double lesson: teacher repeats elements of a fairy tale, pupils write their own fairy tale guided by questions (situation, characters and setting given beforehand)

Teaching Unit	
	– 5th double lesson: pupils read out their stories in changing pairs, then they correct two selected stories (preparation for class test) – 6th double lesson: class test – pupils have to write a tale, guided by 14 questions – 7th double lesson: *Stille Post* – pupils think of a story and tell it to others – 8th double lesson: ten words each for *who* – *where* – *when* – *what* (verbs) – *how* (adjectives) are collected on the board, pupils choose two words from *who*-list and one each from the other lists, then write a 250-word story
Materials:	various fairy tales

Such a time-consuming project means a lot of work for the teacher correcting texts as well as for pupils who have to write, correct and re-write texts. "Trotzdem habe ich dieses Projekt keine Sekunde bereut. Die durchgängige Motivation ... die Neugier auf die entstandenen Geschichten – und wohl auch der Stolz auf das selbst Verfasste – waren so groß, dass wir einige Stunden später, nachdem alle Geschichten abgeschrieben und großenteils wunderschön illustriert waren, noch einmal eine Stunde lang die *nice folders* herumgereicht und gegenseitig bewundert haben" (Tendel 2007:9).

Tasks

1. Betty Reid is a typical example of a bad reader. Read her letter to Dr. Readgood, who is supposed to help her.

   Dear Dr. Readgood,
   My name is Betty Reid. I like talking, dancing, but not reading. I only read when the teacher instructs me to do so – but I never know what for. What I hate most is all the strange words I don't know. So I look up every new word in my dictionary. I take my time reading each word one after the other. To make up for the time lost, I start reading right away,

without thinking what may come. I move my lips when reading silently, fix every single word and often stop to go back to passages read before. Sure I know that reading is easy – you don't need any other knowledge, or any special skills. Please doctor, tell me what's wrong with me – and help me. Regards, Betty Reid

Now slip into Dr. Readgood's role and help Betty to become a good reader. Either write a reply letter starting "Dear Betty ..." or point out all her violations of "The 10 commandments for the active reader".

2. Read the following poem titled *Grass* (1918) by Carl Sandburg (1878 – 1967) and design a 45-minute lesson for a tenth grade. The lesson should primarily aim at students' understanding of the poem, so you may be guided by the *global-to-detail approach* to understanding and analysing literary texts.

Carl Sandburg: GRASS

Pile the bodies high at Austerlitz and Waterloo.
Shovel them under and let me work –
I am the grass; I cover all.

And pile them high at Gettysburg
And pile them high at Ypres and Verdun.
Shovel them under and let me work.
Two years, ten years, and passengers ask the conductor:
What place is this?
Where are we now?

I am the grass.
Let me work.

3. This is the beginning of Margaret Atwood's short story *Happy Endings*, in which she tells the story of John and Mary by offering six different developments. Choose either A, B or C and continue the story.

John and Mary meet.
What happens next?
If you want a happy ending, try A.

A.

John and Mary fall in love and get married.

B.

Mary falls in love with John but John doesn't fall in love with Mary.

C.

John, who is an older man, falls in love with Mary, and Mary, who is only twenty-two, feels sorry for him because he's worried about his hair falling out.

5 Attitudes

5.1 Enjoyment of literature

Reading for information or reading for enjoyment – which is more important?

Reading for enjoyment

People will acquire literary knowledge (chapter 3) and develop literary skills (ch. 4) faster and with a more lasting effect if they feel a certain love of literature. Reading for information is one aim, reading for enjoyment is definitely another vital goal in language classes. Horace's observation *aut prodesse volunt aut delectare poetae* is still true: writers either want to instruct or to please, and literature is *utile* and *dulce*, i.e. useful and sweet. Whether you want to pass the time pleasantly, follow an exciting story, imagine exotic places, share the protagonist's experiences, learn from how he/she deals with moral and psychological problems, get to know various approaches to life and its meaning, study an author's literary skills, or be led to a deeper understanding of yourselves and your fellow human beings – literature provides enjoyment and pleasure.

Lifelong love of books

It goes without saying that a lifetime love of books and reading has numerous benefits. So it is a worthwile attempt to lay the foundations for continuous reading outside and beyond the classroom. Children at school should be encouraged to read as a pleasurable experience, which they go back to again and again. To foster positive attitudes towards literature five areas should be looked at.

Selection

The first is selection. Children can be put off or attracted by reading material, and it is pointless spending time selecting a book if it is never read. The following tips may attract them to reading:

- Choose texts that are suited to your learners.
- In general, look for a well-paced plot, personally relevant content, well-delineated characters, authentic endings, thought-provoking ideas, emotional appeal.
- With young learners, go for simple themes, familiar concepts, simple story-lines, predictable elements, repetitive patterns, short texts, humour, surprise elements, rhythmic language, a good match between text and illustrations (Boothe et al. 1987, Coody 1997).

- Involve pupils in the selection of the text (sense of ownership and responsibility).
- Present alternatives by giving a brief description of each story and organise a class vote for the one pupils like best.
- Try to find the right challenge: too low a level can result in apathy, too high a level can lead to over-anxiety.

Process

Deriving pleasure from reading a book comes from discovering the patterns of plot, the uniqueness of character, the relevance of ideas, the subtleties of language woven into it. This process of discovery can be facilitated by the teacher, who provides time to read, extends the length of time pupils can concentrate, and thus helps them focus on reading books for longer and longer periods. These ideas may contribute to a pleasurable process:

- Enable successful reading experience ... nothing succeeds like success!
- Inform your pupils of why they are asked to read this text.
- Explain the benefits to them.
- Make clear at the beginning how the book is worked on.
- Help them form realistic expectations and avoid frustration by telling them that 100 per cent comprehension is not necessary or possible.
- Create interest in the author of a book being read (Internet research, emailing him/her).
- Present while-reading tasks that really help them in understanding, diversify them, and allow for different forms of response (mixed-level groups).
- Focus on the 4 p's: persons, place, plot, problem.
- Give support and encouragement so that the pupils can overcome the challenge and achieve something.
- Use DEAR (Drop Everything and Read).
- Encourage pupils to think about their approaches to reading.
- Help them make the leap from teacher-guided close study of graded short texts to extensive reading of authentic literature.
- Inform your pupils of a final outcome (response).

Responses

Knowing beforehand that such a final result is expected will increase reading motivation. Demanding responses from readers also rests on the assumption that the more deeply readers are involved the more pleasure they will derive from it. The best response to reading a book is reading another book, however, so post-reading activities should not be over-stressed. Here are a few tips:

- Elicit varied responses to reading.
- Do not always ask them to answer questions in written form.
- Have them talk about books they liked.
- Make them write reviews, which are collected in folders, sold as magazines, or published on the school homepage (or Internet).
- Have students dramatise a favourite scene from a book.
- Convince them of keeping a reading diary (journal, log).
- Encourage self-evaluation: Was the book enjoyable for me? Why (not)? What are my favourite characters? What moments were best? What did I learn?
- Display final outcomes ... to see one's efforts in public is motivating.

Environment

The development of reading enjoyment also depends on the setting and outward circumstances. So teachers are asked to create a print-rich environment that is conducive to reading. These suggestions may help:

- Establish a class library.
- Take good care of your class library (stock, access, display, shelving, ambience, furniture, organisation, support).
- Explore web sites which promote age-related literature.
- Integrate multimedia (television, film tie-ins, audio tapes).
- Organize book talk sessions.
- When reading in lower classes, have props to help with the story.
- Find music to create an atmosphere to go with a book.
- Visit a local publisher.
- Invite the local librarian to talk about books and how to use the library.
- Hold activities to mark national reading initiatives.
- Invite authors, illustrators, storytellers to your school.
- Install a graffiti board where pupils can post book information.

Teacher as role model

Finally, do not forget that the most important factor in creating motivation is you, the teacher. You are the role model for your students, so be a reader yourself, and make clear that you enjoy reading.

- Show your own interest of the ideas, stories, or language in a book being read.
- Read excerpts to your pupils regularly from a variety of good quality fiction.
- Tell them what book you are reading at the moment.
- Bring a pile of your own books into the classroom for pupils to browse.
- Inform your students about recent publications.
- Tell them where they can get quality fiction at low prices.
- Recommend suitable books.

Several of the suggestions above are part of *extensive reading* programmes (Ellis/McRae 1991, Day/Bamford 1998). Stephen Krashen (1994) calls this approach *free voluntary reading* (FVR) and sometimes *pleasure reading*, Hermes (1984) prefers the term *fun reading*.

Extensive reading programmes

While intensive reading with its focus on the teaching of discrete reading skills has its value, the proponents of extensive reading believe that people become good readers through reading. Beyond progress in reading skills, the benefits of such programmes include gains in oral skills, writing proficiency, vocabulary, an increase in motivation and positive affect. "An extensive reading approach aims to get students reading in the second language and liking it" (Day/Bamford 1998: 6).

Extensive reading programme	
amount	reading large quantities
place	in and out of the classroom (classroom library)
material	large selection of books, various genres and topics
selection	by students, including freedom to put down a book they do not like
purpose	enjoyment, pleasure, reading for the sake of reading, content-orientation, information (dependent on individual interest)

language level	grammar and vocabulary should pose no problem, dictionaries should be avoided
mode	individual, silent, autonomous reading
guidance	occasional summaries, mini-presentations or reviews, often no follow-up discussion or work in class
pace	fast (easy material)
teacher's role	organiser, facilitator, role model, individual consulting, keeping record of what they read and like

Moreover the teacher has to get the extensive reading programme off to a good start and explain the benefits of it to the readers. Discovering that they can read in English and that they enjoy it, should stimulate them to read more, which will increase motivation, enjoyment and the desire to read.

Hermes' fun reading

That such a student-centred and student-managed activity can be very successful, has been proven by Hermes (1984) in an overwhelming way: Her 31 first-year learners, who could borrow from 35 readers once a week, read nearly 400 (small) books in five months – that is on average 13 (!) foreign-language readers for each 11-year-old boy or girl. How many English language books had we read when we left school?

Gender gap ...

It has become evident that there is a gender gap in reading. Boys do not seem to like reading as much as girls as they read less and worse. Therefore several initiatives in different countries have been started to make reading a more pleasurable experience for boys in particular. For example, the British Eduaction Secretary has pleaded for boys' bookshelves in schools, as the BBC website reported.

... and a way to bridge it?

Call for boys' own bookshelves

Every secondary school should have a bookshelf of "boys' stories" to try to encourage them to read and close the literacy gap with girls, ministers say.

Education Secretary Alan Johnson said working class boys in particular were falling behind in English lessons. They should be encouraged to read with action and spy stories and to learn by fast-paced, practical lessons, he said. Mr Johnson also announced a

drive to attract more men into teaching in primary schools, to act as role models.
In a speech to the Fabian Society in London, Mr Johnson said by the age of 14, boys were on average 14 percentage points behind girls in their national test results for English. Those from poor homes were doing even less well. "This is the worst possible start for their GCSE years, in which writing skills are so critical," he said. "We need an educational strategy that builds a positive identity for working class boys, instilling in them pride and a love of learning."
He said literacy was crucial to achievement in other subjects. "Boys like books which depict them in powerful roles, often as sporting, spying or fighting heroes – not just Jane Austen, but a necessary dose of Anthony Horowitz as well," he said. "To help get boys reading we need a boys' bookshelf in every secondary school library in the country, containing positive, modern, relevant role models for working class boys."
Parents, he said should turn the television off and read to their children.

http://news.bbc.co.uk/1/hi/education/6451297.stm – 15/03/07

5.2 Sense of quality

What distinguishes 'good' from 'bad' literature?

Aesthetics

A work is said to have *literary merit* if it is a work of quality, if it has some aesthetic value. Such a statement is based on aesthetics, which is a branch of philosophy that studies our sensory-emotional values, investigates our judgments of sentiment and taste, examines what makes something beautiful or ugly, sublime or hilarious, fun or boring, honest or pretentious, discordant or harmonious, humorous or tragic.

Criticism of defining literary merit

Of course, defining literary merit is fraught with dangers and often subjective. *De gustibus non est disputandum* – whether an object of art is aesthetically valuable or valueless is (also) a matter of personal taste. The philosophy of aesthetics has been criticized by post-modernist sociologists and anti-aesthetics as being a relic of a scholarly elite and an expression of an elevated class habitus, and because there is no unique aesthetic object but a broad continuum of cultural forms from ordinary speech to experiences signaled as art by certain institutions.

Benefits of discussing literary merit

Still a critical literary awareness seems to be a desirable goal for our literature students. "Most of the literature produced in the world is of mediocre quality; some of it is bad, some is good, and only a very little is great" (Rotter/Bendl 1981: 245). So it is advisable to develop in our learners a critical attitude towards the quality of texts. Endowed with such an attitude, they can decide more autonomously what to read, and they will appreciate it more profoundly.

Criteria of 'good' literature

What, however, should an evaluation of the quality of literature be based upon? There is obviously a difference between a 'serious' author who believes he has something of lasting value to communicate, and a 'popular' writer, who churns out one book after the other in order to make a lot of money. Yet the matter of literary quality should not be confused with the question of financial reward. What is wrong in a professional writer wanting to earn his living? Sir Walter Scott (1771-1832) produced book after book in order to work off his huge debts, and still his exciting novels possess extraordinary literary qualities.

What then is the basis on which we can we make value judgements in literature? It is definitely not the author's motive that counts but the quality of the work alone. Rotter/Bendl (1981: 245 ff.) suggest several criteria by which we may distinguish 'good' from 'bad' literature.

'Good' literature	'Bad' literature
• It has stood the test of time (problem: decision possible only in retrospect). • A character is true to real life. • The author is aware of the full context, i.e. the complexity of human emotions and the multiplicity of options in conduct and attitude. • He achieves an organic relation among the individual elements of his story. • There is originality in a way that old, unalterable themes are expressed in a new way. • The author is concerned with truth. • Ambiguities in morality and psychology are displayed. • There is multivalence, i.e. in each successive reading one can discover something new.	• The author uses a bestselling formula appealing to a wide readership. • Stock characters or stereotypes are employed. • He presents a world of black and white. • He avoids complex issues. • He reduces the range of human emotions. • He is not concerned with the psychological basis of action. • He tries to flatter the readers' moral sense. • The focus is on a fast-moving narrative. • Cheap dramatic effects are important. • Credibility of plot and character are sacrificed for violent effect and emotional opportunism.

Developing a sense of quality

To put it into a nutshell, 'good' literature, according to Rotter/Bendl, is characterized by six features: quality of permanence, awareness of full context, organic unity, originality, concern with truth, and multivalence. This summary or the statements in the table above, though each of them may be cast into doubt, can be presented in class after a literary text has been read. A critical discussion of the criteria themselves as well as a comparison between the criteria and the text can make learners develop a certain sense of – or feeling for – the quality of literature.

5.3 Intercultural awareness

What has literature got to do with intercultural learning?

Literature and intercultural learning

In the 1990s people began to see the potential of literature for intercultural learning (Kramsch 1993, Bredella 2002, Delanoy 2002, Müller-Hartmann/Schocker-von Ditfurth 2004). Language and culture are inseparable, and foreign literature represents linguistic and cultural otherness. When our students read a foreign text, they experience other value systems and are forced to compare the home and foreign identities in a process of intercultural learning. "In the process of relating their own values and world view(s) to those of the text, comparing and contrasting them, learners might change and co-ordinate perspectives and thus begin to understand the other culture" (Müller-Hartmann/Schocker-von Ditfurth 2004: 123). So teaching foreign literature can arouse curiosity and openness towards the other culture, ask the readers to decentre from their own positions, force them to change perspectives, make them reflect on auto- and hetero-stereotypes, all of which may lead to a better understanding between different cultures.

Kramsch's Third Place

If we follow Claire Kramsch (1993), reading foreign literature may lead us to the *Third Place*. When learners' understanding of a foreign language develops they may come to understand other values which are familiar to the foreign culture, but alien to their own culture. Nevertheless their understanding of these values is still different to that of the native speaker. So foreign language learning takes place in a *Third Place*, which the learner must make for him/herself between their first culture (C1) and the foreign language culture (C2). They must try to adopt four perspectives – how members of the foreign culture see themselves (C2 – C2), how they see us and our culture (C2 – C1), how we see the foreign culture and their members (C1 – C2), and how we see ourselves (C1 – C1). This involves the learners in a constant reflection of C1 and C2, and as they choose those meanings that best reflect their personal perspectives, individual interpretations of culture rather than rigid stereotypical notions are promoted.

Suitable texts and tasks

To facilitate this process, literary texts should be selected which tell about the lives of (young) people from other cultures, including the whole field of children's and young adult literature. Intercultural conflicts and causes for misunderstanding are particularly dramatised in post-colonial literature and minority texts. Moreover texts written by learners from other cultures can be studied – and compared with one's own texts. Such interactive projects may take the form of e-mail exchanges between classes in two different countries, discussing the same literary text from two cultural points of view. So the choice of a suitable text must be accompanied by setting tasks that "facilitate negotiation of meaning between the foreign culture represented in the text and the learners' own culture" (Müller-Hartmann/Schocker-von Ditfurth 2004: 123).

An example: *Germans at Meat*

To foster intercultural awareness, teachers may also use a text written by a member of C2 that deals with one's own culture (C1). In Katherine Mansfield's amusing short story *Germans at Meat*, the middle-class Germans before World War I are the object of her satire. A close reading and appropriate follow-up tasks can explore all four perspectives. Analysing content, theme and form shows how the (British) narrator assesses the German culture – obsession by food, lack of decency, boastfulness etc. (C2 – C1). It will also make clear how she sees her own culture, not only regarding tea (C2 – C2). Learners can be asked whether they share Herr Rat's opinions of the British (C1 – C2). They can also be encouraged to reflect on Frau Stiegelauer's and Herr Rat's behaviour and attitudes (C1 – C1).

Katherine Mansfield: ***Germans at Meat*** *(first third of text)*

Bread soup was placed upon the table.
"Ah," said the Herr Rat, leaning upon the table as he peered into the tureen, "that is what I need. My 'magen' has not been in order for several days. Bread soup, and just the right consistency. I am a good cook myself" – he turned to me.
"How interesting," I said, attempting to infuse just the right amount of enthusiasm into my voice.
"Oh yes – when one is not married it is necessary. As for me, I have had all I wanted from women without marriage."
He tucked his napkin into his collar and blew upon his soup as he spoke. "Now at nine o'clock I make myself an English breakfast, but not much. Four slices of bread, two eggs, two slices of cold ham, one plate of soup, two cups of tea – that is nothing to you."
He asserted the fact so vehemently that I had not the courage to refute it.
All eyes were suddenly turned upon me. I felt I was bearing the burden of the nation's preposterous breakfast – I who drank a cup of coffee while buttoning my blouse in the morning.
"Nothing at all," cried Herr Hoffman from Berlin. "Ach, when I was in England in the morning I used to eat."
He turned up his eyes and his moustache, wiping the soup drippings from his coat and waistcoat.
"Do they really eat so much?" asked Fraulein Stiegelauer.
"Soup and baker's bread and pig's flesh, and tea and coffee and stewed fruit, and honey and eggs, and cold fish and kidneys, and hot fish and liver. All the ladies eat, too, especially the ladies?"
"Certainly. I myself have noticed it, when I was living in a hotel in Leicester Square," cried the Herr Rat. "It was a good hotel, but they could not make tea – now –"
"Ah, that's one thing I can do," said I, laughing brightly, "I can make very good tea. The great secret is to warm the teapot."
"Warm the teapot," interrupted the Herr Rat, pushing away his soup plate. "What do you warm the teapot for? Ha! ha! that's very good! One does not eat the teapot, I suppose?"
He fixed his cold blue eyes upon me with an expression which suggested a thousand premeditated invasions.
"So that is the great secret of your English tea? All you do is to warm the teapot."

I wanted to say that was only the preliminary canter, but could not translate it, and so was silent.
The servant brought in veal, with "sauerkraut" and potatoes.
"I eat sauerkraut with great pleasure," said the Traveller from North Germany, "but now I have eaten so much of it that I cannot retain it. I am immediately forced to –"
"A beautiful day," I cried, turning to Fraulein Stiegelauer. "Did you get up early?"
"At five o'clock I walked for ten minutes in the wet grass. Again in bed. At half-past five I fell asleep, and woke at seven, when I made an 'over-body' washing! Again in bed. At eight o'clock I had a cold-water poultice, and at half-past eight I drank a cup of mint tea. At nine I drank some malt coffee, and began my 'cure.' Pass me the sauerkraut, please. You do not eat it?"
"No, thank you. I still find it a little strong."

From: Mansfield, Katherine: In a German Pension, 1911

Empathy

Such inter-cultural learning involves intra-cultural awareness and empathy in general. Readers learn how people can talk about what they think, want and feel. They learn that another person feels differently about something to what they are used to – a different love, a different hatred. Philosophy professor Peter Bieri put it this way: "Er kann, weil sein begriffliches Repertoire größer geworden ist, nuancierter über sein Erleben reden, und das wiederum ermöglicht ihm, differenzierter zu empfinden" (Bieri 2007: 27).

Tasks

1. Look back at how to encourage a positive attitude towards literature. Then reflect on how the following aphorisms relate to these various ways:
   a) Readers are made by readers.
   b) The second best way to learn a foreign language is extensive reading.
   c) Reading is like an infectious disease. It is caught, not taught. (Nuttall)
   d) Teachers must encourage pupils to want to read.
   e) People learn to read, and to read better, by reading. (Eskey)

2. What is your opinion of the British Education Secretary's plea for special boys' bookshelves in classrooms?
3. Popular writers who produce one bestseller after the other are very often not regarded as serious authors, and their products called literary trash. What could be the reasons for their enormous commercial success then?
4. The New York Times reviewed the new bestseller by French literature professor Pierre Bayard, *How to Talk About Books You Haven't Read*? What do you think of his attitude and suggestions?

Read It? No, but You Can Skim a Few Pages and Fake It

PARIS, Feb. 23 — It may well be that too many books are published, but by good fortune, not all must be read. In practice, primed by publishers, critics, teachers, authors and word-of-mouth, a form of natural selection limits essential reading to those classics and best sellers that become part of civilized intellectual and social discourse.

Of course, many people don't get through these books, either, and too embarrassed to admit it, they worry constantly about being exposed as philistines. Now Pierre Bayard, a Paris University literature professor, has come to their rescue with a survivor's guide to life in the chattering classes. And it is evidently much in need. "How to Talk About Books You Haven't Read?" has become a best seller here, with translation rights snapped up across Europe and under negotiation in Britain and the United States. "I am surprised because I hadn't imagined how guilty nonreaders feel," Mr. Bayard, 52, said in an interview. "With this book, they can shake off their guilt without psychoanalysis, so it's much cheaper."

Mr. Bayard reassures them that there is no obligation to read, and confesses to lecturing students on books that he has either not read or has merely skimmed. And he recalls passionate exchanges with people who also have not read the book under discussion.

He further cites writers like Montaigne, who could not remember what he read, and Paul Valéry, who found ways of praising authors whose books he had never opened. Mr. Bayard finds characters in novels by Graham Greene, David Lodge and others who cheerfully question the need to read at all. And he refuses to be intimidated by Proust or Joyce. Having demonstrated that non-readers are in good company, Mr. Bayard then offers tips on how to cover up ignorance of a "must-read" book. ... Students, he noted from experience, are skilled at opining about books they have not read, building on elements he may have provided in a lecture. This approach can also work in the more exposed arena of social gatherings: the book's cover, reviews and other public reaction to it, gossip about the author and even the current conversation can all provide food for sounding informed.

One alternative, he said, is to try to change the subject. Another is to admit not knowing a particular book while suggesting knowledge of the so-called "collective library" into which the book fits.

But Mr. Bayard's most daring suggestion is that nonreaders should talk about themselves, using the pretext of the book without dwelling on its contents. In this way, he said, they are forced to tap their imagination and, in effect, invent their own book. "To be able to talk with finesse about something one does not know is worth more than the universe of books," he writes.

www.nytimes.com/2007/02/24/books/24read.htm 24/02/07

Genres

6 Shorties

6.1 Types of short narrative forms

What kinds of short narrative texts do you know, apart from short stories?

Benefits of shorties

To state the obvious, short narrative forms are good teaching material because they are short and narrative (Thaler 2015). Due to their relative brevity, they are flexible in use, and can often be dealt with in a single 45-minute lesson. And telling a story serves many functions – as a means of making sense of an individual's experiences, a medium of communication and community, a form of entertainment, a source of solace, a fundamental need: "So while we live with the anxiety that our lives may have one of these key attributes but not the other (they come to an end, but they do not make sense), we comfort ourselves with narratives, which have both these desiderata: they have beginnings, middles and ends, and they make sense" (Toolan 2001: 14). Beyond those anthropological, psychological and social needs, stories fulfil moral, pedagogic, and methodological functions.

Variety of forms

It is no wonder then that story telling is an omnipresent phenomenon – in everyday life, the media, and the classroom. There are a wealth of different narrative texts – from traditional simple forms (fairy tales, fables, legends), which are characterised by simple plot and diction as well as oral telling style, to more complex narrative genres (short stories) and modern media forms (sitcoms, news stories, hyperfiction). The following diagram demonstrates the variety of short narrative forms (Thaler 2015).

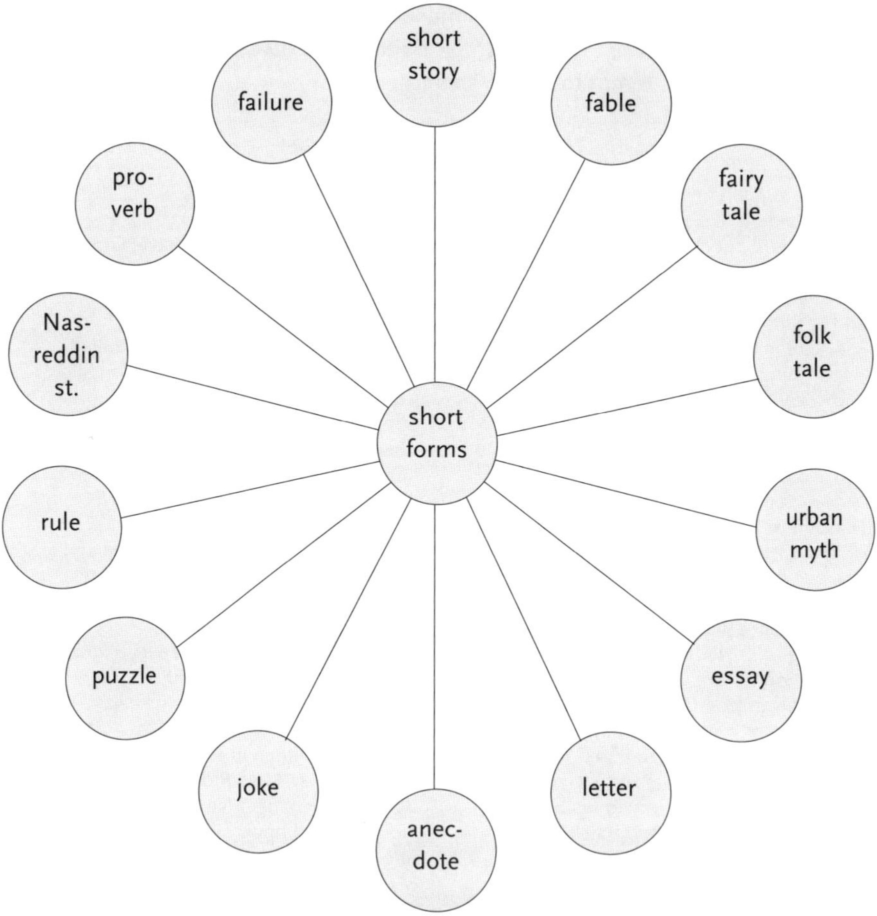

Fairy tale parodies

One of the traditional forms is the popular *fairy tale*, which has also provoked the creation of parodies on it. A *parody*, also called *spoof* in its light, playful version, is a work that imitates another work in order to ridicule the work, its subject or author – or as literary theorist Linda Hutcheon puts it, "imitation with a critical difference, not always at the expense of the parodied text" (2000: 7). Parodies have been part of English culture from Geoffrey Chaucer's *Canterbury Tales* (Sir Thopas) to post-modern pastiche and *Uncyclopedia*, an online parody of Wikipedia. In the classroom, they are fun, make canonical works accessible to larger audiences by presenting them humorously (e.g. Shakespeare's

Hamlet by The Simpsons), and contribute to student writing, when learners study, imitate and alter academic forms in an attempt to master them.

Little Red Riding Hood – a spoof

As soon as Wolf began to feel
That he would like a decent meal,
He went and knocked on Grandma's door.
When Grandma opened it, she saw
The sharp white teeth, the horrid grin,
And Wolfie said, "May I come in?"
Poor Grandmamma was terrified,
"He's going to eat me up!" she cried.
And she was absolutely right.
He ate her up in one big bite.
But Grandmamma was small and tough,
And Wolfie wailed, "That's not enough!
I haven't yet begun to feel
That I have had a decent meal!"'
He ran around the kitchen yelping,
"I've *got* to have a second helping!"
Then added with a frightful leer,
"I'm therefore going to wait right here
Till Little Miss Red Riding Hood
Comes home from walking in the wood."
He quickly put on Grandma's clothes,
(Of course he hadn't eaten those).
He dressed himself in coat and hat.
He put on shoes, and after that
He even brushed and curled his hair,
Then sat himself in Grandma's chair.
In came the little girl in red.
She stopped. She stared. And then she said,
"What great big ears you have, Grandma."
"All the better to hear you with," the Wolf
replied.
"What great big eyes you have, Grandma."
said Little Red Riding Hood.
"All the better to see you with,"
the Wolf replied.
He sat there watching her and smiled.
He thought, I'm going to eat this child.
Compared with her old Grandmamma
She's going to taste like caviar.
Then Little Red Riding Hood said,
"But Grandma,
what a lovely great big furry coat you
have on."
"That's wrong!" cried Wolf. "Have you forgot
To tell me what BIG TEETH I've got?
Ah well, no matter what you say,
I'm going to eat you anyway."
The small girl smiles. One eyelid flickers.
She wimps a pistol from her knickers.
She aims it at the creature's head
And *bang bang bang*, she shoots him dead.
A few weeks later, in the wood,
I came across Miss Riding Hood.
But what a change! No cloak of red,
No silly hood upon her head.
She said, "Hello, and do please note
My lovely furry wolfskin coat."

Anecdotes

An *anecdote* is a brief tale which narrates an interesting or amusing biographical incident. It is based on real life, involving actual people, in real places, but due to retelling often becomes a fictional piece, which is "too good to be true". Although usually humorous, the aim of an anecdote is not only to evoke laughter, but to reveal some general truth, to unveil the workings of an institution, or to delineate a character trait.

A famous anecdote on Winston Churchill

Lady Astor once remarked to Winston Churchill
at a dinner party:
"If I were your wife I would poison your tea."
Without showing any agitation Churchill replied:
"If I were your husband I would drink it."

Mini-sagas

A *mini-saga* is a text that consists of exactly 50 words – plus a title which must not be longer than 15 words. It tells a story with a beginning, a middle and an end, but does not necessarily have to be in prose. Its brevity forces the writers to reduce and compress their means of expression. The English language with its short words lends itself neatly to this dense form of writing, and this genre is very popular in Great Britain. The first mini-sagas appeared in 1982 in *The Sunday Telegraph*, when it started to hold a competition for the best ones. Mini-sagas provide an excellent vehicle for a short writing lesson because they are easy to read and understand, writing fifty words does not sound too difficult to the learner, they can be very motivating, and they also focus on accuracy (in the editing stage). Given a few guidelines and examples, students often come up with really creative texts.

A mini-saga

Like mother, like son
1955
Dear Mummy,
I hate this boarding school. Food awful, prefects bully me.
Please take me home.
Love, David ---
Dear David,
Nonsense! Chin up. – Mother
1997
Dear David,
I hate this Home. Food awful, nurses treat me like a child.
Fetch me immediately. – Mother ---
Dear Mother,
Nonsense! Chin up. – David

Nasreddin stories

Nasreddin stories are centred around Nasreddin, a satirical Sufi figure who lived somewhere in the Near or Middle East around the 13th century. Most of his actions are both illogical and logical, bizarre and normal, simple and profound. What adds to his uniqueness is how he gets across his messages in unconventional yet effective ways. Nasreddin stories are also adapted and used as teaching stories by followers of Sufism. As there are usually several layers of meaning, Nasreddin stories are open to multiple interpretations.

Two Nasreddin stories

1. An admirer of his once asked the sage: "Master, why did you never marry?" "Well," he replied, "In my youth I searched for the perfect woman. I spent time with many women, but they all had a flaw. One would be beautiful, but cruel. Another intelligent, but lazy. I had almost given up hope, when I met her, the perfect woman. Healthy, intelligent, sensitive, witty, beautiful, talented ... she was everything I was looking for."
"So why did you not marry her?"
"Odd thing," replied the Hoja,
"She was looking for the perfect man."

2. One of the neighbours found Nasreddin scattering crumbs all around his house.
"Why are you doing that?" he asked. –
"I'm keeping the tigers away," replied Nasreddin.
"But there aren't any tigers round here," said the neighbour.
"That's right," said Nasreddin. "You see how well it works?"

Jokes

Another short and humorous form of narrative is the *joke*. It lasts just a few seconds or minutes, and can be used as an introduction to a lesson, a starting point for a discussion or creative activity, a way to relax the students and prepare them for more serious work, a pleasant conclusion of a lesson, and a medium of intercultural learning – with insights into a nation's humour and culture, including stereotypes and clichés.

An intercultural joke

On a group of beautiful deserted islands in the middle of nowhere, the following people are stranded:

2 Italian men and 1 Italian woman
2 French men and 1 French woman
2 German men and 1 German woman
2 English men and 1 English woman
2 Japanese men and 1 Japanese woman
2 Chinese men and 1 Chinese woman
2 American men and 1 American woman
2 Irish men and 1 Irish woman

One month later on these absolutely stunning deserted islands in the middle of nowhere, the following things have occurred:

One Italian man killed the other Italian man for the Italian woman.
The two French men and the French woman are living happily together in menage-a-trois.
The two German men have a strict weekly schedule of alternating visits with the German woman.
The two English men are waiting for someone to introduce them to the English woman.
The two Japanese have faxed Tokyo and are awaiting instructions.
The two Chinese men have set up a pharmacy /liquor store / restaurant/laundry, and have got the woman pregnant in order to supply employees for their store.
The two American men are contemplating the virtues of suicide because the American woman keeps on complaining about her body, the true nature of feminism, how she can do everything they can do, the necessity of fulfilment, the equal division of household chores, how sand and palm trees make her look fat, how her last boyfriend respected her opinion and treated her nicer than they do, and how her relationship with her mother is improving, and how at least the taxes are low and it isn't raining.
The two Irishmen divided the island into North and South, and set up a distillery. They do not remember if sex is in the picture because it gets sort of foggy after the first few litres of coconut whiskey. But they're satisfied because at least the English aren't having any fun.

Puzzles

A genre that is even shorter than a joke is the *puzzle*. Riddles, brain teasers or puzzles help to explore linguistic features, train the brain and have a competitive edge.

Two linguistic puzzles

– *What do you say to King Kong when he gets married?*
– *If your mum comes from Iceland and your dad from Cuba, then what are you?*

Proverbs …

Of similar brevity is the *proverb* (seven words on average). "A proverb is a short, generally known sentence of the folk which contains wisdom, truth, morals, and traditional views in a metaphorical, fixed and memorizable form and which is handed down from generation to generation" (Mieder 1989: 119). Subgenres include proverbial expressions ("to bite the dust"), proverbial comparisons ("as busy as a bee"), and wellerisms, named after Sam Weller from Charles Dickens's The Pickwick Papers (1837), constructed in a triadic manner, with a statement (often a proverb), an identification of a speaker, and a phrase that places the statement into an unexpected situation ("Every evil is followed by some good," as the man said when his wife died the day after he became bankrupt). Proverbs lend themselves to stylistic analysis, as they often contain rhetorical figures (thus placing this genre also into poetic texts: see 8) such as rhyme (When the cat is away, the mice will play), alliteration (Forgive and forget), parallelism (Nothing ventured, nothing gained), ellipsis (Once bitten, twice shy), personification (Hunger is the best cook), hyperbole (All is fair in love and war), or paradox (The longest way around is the shortest way home).

… and anti-proverbs

The transformation of a proverb in order to cause a humorist effect is called *anti-proverb*. There are several formal and thematic devices to construct (or analyse) such anti-proverbs, for example reduction, supplementation, substitution, contrast, or synthesis.

Anti-proverbs

– All's well that ends. (reduction)
– A barking dog never bites, but a lot of dogs don't know this proverb. (supplementation)
– The best things in life are for a fee. (substitution)
– All we need is love – all we get is homework. (contrast)
– Duty is calling? We call back. (break of metaphor)
– Marriages are made in heaven knows what state of mind. (synthesis)

Quotes and twisted quotes

A form that is similar to proverbs and anti-proverbs is the *quote* or *twisted quote*. In the latter a plain statement is combined with a strange addition, or an everyday situation gets an unexpected twist.

Twisted quotes

– A terrible thing happened again last night – nothing. (Phyllis Diller)
– My interest is in the future because I'm going to spend the rest of my life there. (C.F. Kettering)
– Somebody is boring me; I think it's me. (Dylan Thomas)

Letters

Reading and writing *letters* has been part of English classrooms for a long time. One usually distinguishes between formal and informal letters, personal and business letters (plus letters to the editor). The digital era has added the Email, and another sub-genre is made up of (humorous) answers to letters.

Answers to children's letters from Santa

1. Dear Mike,
I think you take some of the spirit out of Christmas when you ask for "Cash – or else!" – Yours truly, Santa

2. Dear Pamela,
Santa only brings presents. I'm afraid I cannot take away your baby brother. – Love, Santa

Rules *Rules* are an integral element of life and school. So-called *fumblerules* can be employed by English teachers to get across the correct usage of English grammar. Each fumblerule describes an error of style or grammar while simultaneously providing an example of this error.

William Safire's Fumblerules

1. *Avoid run-on sentences they are hard to read.*
2. *Don't use no double negatives.*
3. *Use the semicolon properly, always use it where it is appropriate; and never where it isn't.*
4. *Reserve the apostrophe for it's proper use and omit it when its not needed.*
5. *Do not put statements in the negative form.*
6. *Verbs has to agree with their subjects.*
7. *No sentence fragments.*
8. *Proofread carefully to see if you any words out.*
9. *Avoid commas, that are not necessary.*
10. *If you reread your work, you will find on rereading that a great deal of repetition can be avoided by rereading and editing.*
11. *A writer must not shift your point of view.*
12. *Eschew dialect, irregardless.*
13. *And don't start a sentence with a conjunction.*
14. *Don't overuse exclamation marks!!!*
15. *Place pronouns as close as possible, especially in long sentences, as of 10 or more words, to their antecedents.*
16. *Hyphenate between sy-llables and avoid un-necessary hyphens.*
17. *Write all adverbial forms correct.*
18. *Don't use contractions in formal writing.*
19. *Writing carefully, dangling participles must be avoided.*
20. *It is incumbent on us to avoid archaisms.*
21. *If any word is improper at the end of a sentence, a linking verb is.*
22. *Steer clear of incorrect forms of verbs that have snuck in the language.*
23. *Take the bull by the hand and avoid mixed metaphors.*
24. *Avoid trendy locutions that sound flaky.*
25. *Never, ever use repetitive redundancies.*
26. *Everyone should be careful to use a singular pronoun with singular nouns in their writing.*

27. *If I've told you once, I've told you a thousand times, resist hyperbole.*
28. *Also avoid awkward or affected alliteration.*
29. *Don't string too many prepositional phrases together unless you are walking through the valley of the shadow of death.*
30. *Always pick on the correct idiom.*
31. *"Avoid overuse of 'quotation "marks."'"*
32. *Last but not least, avoid clichés like the plague.*

Failures

Failures like the fumblerules above are always a source of humour. Mistakes and errors in learner texts can take on the form of stylistic howlers. It is a rewarding task to ask students to spot the howler and correct it.

Stylistic howlers on Shakespeare

Shakespeare was born in 1564, supposedly on his birthday. He never made much money and is famous only because of his plays. He lived in Windsor with his merry wives, writing tragedies, comedies and errors, all in Islamic pentameter. Romeo and Juliet are an example of heroic couplet. The next great author, John Milton, wrote Paradise Lost. Then his wife died and he wrote Paradise Regained.

6.2 Teaching techniques

Apart from interpretation, how would you work with a short narrative text in class?

Narrative competence

Narrative texts are different from dramatic and lyric texts. So when using narrative texts in class an important goal must be to develop *narrative competence*. Students should know the rules and conventions of stories in order to understand and appreciate them, and also to be able to produce their own narrative texts – in oral and written forms. "Wenn Lernende sich kompetent und kritisch mit den privaten und öffentlichen *stories* auseinander setzen sollen, denen sie im Alltag und in den Medien auf Schritt und Tritt begegnen, dann müssen sie zunächst einmal die Elemente, Strukturen und Mechanismen kennen lernen, die in die Konstruktion von Erzählungen eingehen" (Nünning/Surkamp 2006:199).

Conventions of oral telling

The sociolinguist William Labov has put forward six basic rules or conventions of an oral story (cf. Toolan 2001: 148).

Conventions of oral telling (Labov)	
1. Abstract:	What, in a nutshell, is this story about?
2. Orientation:	Who, when, where?
3. Complicating action:	What happened and then what happened?
4. Evaluation:	So what?
5. Result (resolution):	What finally happened?
6. Coda:	That's it, I've finished and am 'bridging' back to our present situation.

Herringbone technique

When reading or writing a story, students must be able to identify and organize important story elements and observe relationships between them. A useful technique for analysing a single idea or text is the *herringbone technique*, so-named because it resembles a fish skeleton. This graphic organizer provides students with a structure by asking of the main idea the six questions: Who? What? When? Where? Why? How?

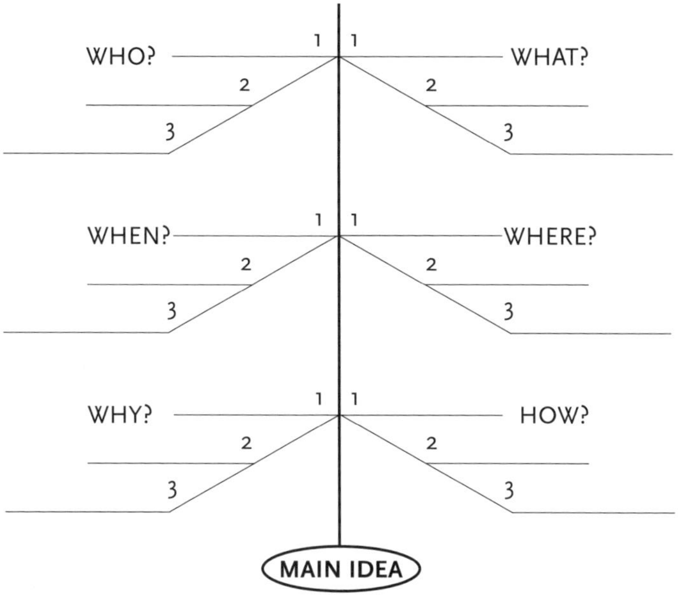

Constituents of story and discourse

It seems reasonable to distinguish between story and discourse. Whereas story means the succession of events in its chronological order, discourse refers to the structure of narrative transmission and the way the story is presented by the narrator. When analysing a narrative text, at least the following main constituents should be covered:

- Events, actions
- Characters
- Setting: time, place
- Narrator
- Point of view

Creative approaches

Working with narrative texts should, however, not be reduced to analysing the different categories. Creative, process and product oriented approaches including writing and telling one's own stories must be added. "Neben den ... kognitiv-analytischen Kategorien und Zugangsweisen bedarf es jedoch der Ergänzung durch weitere, schülerzentrierte, kreative und produktionsorientierte Methoden, die für die Ausbildung von aktiver narrativer Kompetenz unverzichtbar sind" (Nünning/Surkamp 2006: 199).

Maley's 12 procedures

If teachers want to put this imperative into practice, they can resort to Alan Maley, who has collected 12 generalisable procedures for texts in an inspiring book with the telling name *Short and Sweet* (1995).

Maley's 12 procedures for short texts

Procedure	*Examples*
1. Expansion	• Add one or more sentences • Add certain words (e.g. adjectives) • Add comment within the text
2. Reduction	• Remove specified items (e.g. adjectives) • Remove sentences • Turn it into telegraphese
3. Media transfer	• Transfer it into visuals (e.g. pictures) • Turn it into a poem • Turn it into a radio play
4. Matching	• Match text with a title • Match text with another text • Match text with a visual representation
5. Selection/ranking	• Choose the best text for a certain purpose (e.g. inclusion in a teen mag) • Choose the text closest to the original
6. Comparison/contrast	• Identify words / ideas / rhetorical devices common to both texts • Identify items present in one text only
7. Reconstruction	• Reorder jumbled words / lines / sentences / paragraphs • Fill in gaps
8. Reformulation	• Rewrite in a different style / mood • Retell written text orally • Use keywords to rewrite it
9. Interpretation	• What's the meaning? • What personal connections does it have? • What does the text not say?
10. Creating text	• Write a parallel text on a different theme • Use the same title but write a new text • Use 10 words from the text and write s.th. new
11. Analysis	• Study the use of tenses • What verbs are used? • How many ... does the text contain?
12. Project work	• Use the text for an advertising campaign • Design a questionnaire • Prepare a brief magazine article

6.3 Short stories

Which of the short stories you read at school do you remember best? Why?

Popularity of short story

The genre of short stories deserves a sub-chapter of its own because of its long-standing curricular importance. Each TEFL publisher has several anthologies of suitable short stories plus model interpretations or lesson plans. One reason why the short story has been a popular text type in many classrooms for a long time now may be that due to its brevity and literary aesthetics it serves as a bridge between simpler coursebook texts and full-length Literature with a capital L masterpieces.

Definition

It is generally believed to be impossible to find a definition that fits the diversity of this genre. The first theorist of the short story, E.A. Poe, demanded that in "a brief prose tale" each word or incident be aimed at "a certain single effect" and that the story must be short enough to "be read at one sitting" to guarantee true unity and the "preconceived effect" (Galloway 1980: 445f.). The main features of this fictitious narrative in prose which is shorter and less complex than a novel may be summarised as follows (Werlich 1999):

- It centres around one *incident*, which is often revealed as an unusual one.
- It organizes character and action into a simple *plot* (*plot stories* vs *plotless stories*), focusing on a single turning-point or a surprising reversal.
- It concentrates on a limited number of *characters*, often revealing their state of mind at some single moment of crisis and presenting a clash of characters
- It is often confined to one *setting*, covering in detail only a short period of time.
- It is told in *language* highly charged with meaning and suggestion, enhanced by the repetition of key words and leitmotifs.
- It builds up *suspense* towards the end (denouément).

Example: *You Were Perfectly Fine*

These six characteristics may be studied in a fine example of sophisticated *New Yorker* wit, Dorothy Parker's brief vignette *You Were Perfectly Fine*, which gives us a swift insight into the *lost generation* of the jazz age.

Dorothy Parker: ***You Were Perfectly Fine***

The pale young man eased himself carefully into the low chair, and rolled his head to the side, so that the cool chintz comforted his cheek and temple.
"Oh, dear," he said. "Oh, dear, oh, dear, oh, dear. Oh."
The clear-eyed girl, sitting light and erect on the couch, smiled brightly at him.
"Not feeling so well today?" she said.
"Oh, I'm great," he said. "Corking, I am. Know what time I got up? Four o'clock this afternoon, sharp. I kept trying to make it, and every time I took my head off the pillow, it would roll under the bed. This isn't my head I've got on now. I think this is something that used to belong to Walt Whitman. Oh, dear, oh, dear, oh, dear."
"Do you think maybe a drink would make you feel better?" she said.
"The hair of the mastiff that bit me?" he said. "Oh, no, thank you. Please never speak of anything like that again. I'm through. I'm all, all through. Look at that hand; steady as a hummingbird. Tell me, was I very terrible last night?"
"Oh, goodness," she said, "everybody was feeling pretty high. You were all right."
"Yeah," he said. "I must have been dandy. Is everybody sore at me?"
"Good heavens, no," she said. "Everyone thought you were terribly funny. Of course, Jim Pierson was a little stuffy, there for a minute at dinner. But people sort of held him back in his chair, and got him calmed down. I don't think anybody at the other tables noticed at all. Hardly anybody."
"He was going to sock me?" he said. "Oh, Lord. What did I do to him?"
"Why, you didn't do a thing," she said. "You were perfectly fine. But you know how silly Jim gets when he thinks anybody is making too much fuss over Elinor."
"Was I making a pass at Elinor?" he said. "Did I do that?"
"Of course you didn't," she said. "You were only fooling, that's all. She thought you were awfully amusing. She was having a marvelous time. She only got a little tiny bit annoyed just once, when you poured the clam juice down her back."
"My God," he said. "Clam juice down that back. And every

vertebra a little Cabot. What'll I ever do?"
"Oh, she'll be all right," she said. "Just send her some flowers or something. Don't worry about it. It isn't anything."
"No, I won't worry," he said. "I haven't got a care in the world. I'm sitting pretty. Oh, dear, oh, dear. Did I do any other fascinating tricks at dinner?"
"You were fine," she said. "Don't be so foolish about it. Everybody was crazy about you. The owner was a little worried because you wouldn't stop singing, but he really didn't mind. All he said was, he was afraid they'd close the place again, if there was so much noise. But he didn't care a bit, himself. I think he loved seeing you have such a good time. Oh, you were just singing away there, for about an hour. It wasn't so terribly loud, at all."
"So I sang," he said. "That must have been a treat. I sang."
"Don't you remember?" she said. "You sang one song after another. Everybody in the place was listening. They loved it. Only you kept insisting that you wanted to sing some song about some kind of fusiliers or other, and everybody kept shushing you, and you'd keep trying to start it again. You were wonderful. We were all trying to make you stop singing for a minute, and eat something, but you wouldn't hear of it. My, you were funny."
"Didn't I eat any dinner?" he said.
"Oh, not a thing," she said. "Every time the waiter would offer you something, you'd give it right back to him because you said that he was your long-lost brother, changed in the cradle by a gypsy band, and that anything you had was his. You had him simply roaring at you."
"I bet I did," he said. "I bet I was comical. Society's Pet, I must have been. And what happened then, after my overwhelming success with the waiter?"
"Why, nothing much," she said. "You took a sort of dislike to some old man with white hair, sitting across the room, because you didn't like his necktie, and you wanted to tell him about it. But we got you out before he got really mad."
"Oh, we got out," he said. "Did I walk?"
"Walk! Of course you did," she said. "You were absolutely all right. There was that nasty stretch of ice on the sidewalk, and you did sit down awfully hard, you poor dear. But good heavens, that might have happened to anybody."
"Oh, sure," he said. "Louisa Alcott or anybody. So I fell down on

the sidewalk. That would explain what's the matter with my -- Yes, I see. And then what, if you don't mind?"
"Ah, now, Peter!" she said. "You can't sit there and say you don't remember what happened after that! I did think that maybe you were just a little tight at dinner -- Oh, you were perfectly all right, and all that, but I did know you were feeling pretty gay. But you were so serious, from the time that you fell down -- I never knew you to be that way. Don't you know, how you told me I had never seen your real self before? Oh, Peter, I just couldn't bear it, if you didn't remember that lovely long ride we took together in the taxi! Please, you do remember that, don't you? I think it would simply kill me, if you didn't."
"Oh, yes," he said. "Riding in the taxi. Oh, yes, sure. Pretty long ride, hmm?"
"Round and round the park," she said. "Oh and the trees were shining so in the moonlight. And you said you never knew before that you really had a soul."
"Yes," he said. "I said that. That was me."
"You said such lovely things," she said. "And I'd never known, all this time, how you had been feeling about me, and I'd never dared to let you see how I felt about you. And then last night -- oh, Peter dear, I think that taxi ride was the most important thing that ever happened to us in our lives."
"Yes," he said. "I guess it must have been."
"And we're going to be so happy," she said. "Oh, I just want to tell everybody! But I don't know -- I think maybe it would be sweeter to keep it all to ourselves."
"I think it would be," he said.
"Isn't it lovely?" she said.
"Yes," he said. "Great."
"Lovely!" she said.
"Look here," he said. "Do you mind if I have a drink? I mean, just medicinally, you know. I'm off the stuff for life, so help me. But I think I feel a collapse coming on."
"Oh, I think it would do you good," she said. "You poor boy. It's a shame you feel so awful. I'll go make you a whiskey and soda."
"Honestly," he said. "I don't see how you could ever want to speak to me again, after I made such a fool of myself last night. I think I'd better go join a monastery in Tibet."
"You crazy idiot!" she said. "As if I could ever let you go away now!

Stop talking like that. You were perfectly fine!"
She jumped up from the couch, kissed him quickly on the forehead, and ran out of the room.
The pale young man looked after her and shook his head long and slowly, then dropped it in his damp and trembling hands.
"Oh, dear," he said. "Oh, dear, oh, dear, oh, dear."

Multitude of story types

Of course, not all short stories fit Poe's or Werlich's definitions as the genre itself has gone through a long development. The *plot story* of the 19th century (Poe, Irving, Hawthorne) with a single motive, a tightly-knit plot (abrupt opening, turning-point, surprise ending) and the unity of effect may be seen as the first or classical type of the short story, but not the only one (Rotter/ Bendl 1981: 77ff.). It remained very popular until 1920, but the 20th century saw many new trends. The *formula* or *magazine story* (*O. Henryism*) was a product of commercialization, mechanically following the conventional structure, with truth sacrificed to effect, stereotyped and sterile (many Westerns, Jerry Cotton stories). The psychological, *impressionistic*, lyrical *slice-of-life story* (1920 – 1940) does not aim at a clear structure or plot, but is limited to a fully explored moment of time, often using the stream-of-consciousness technique (Anderson, Mansfield, Woolf). In its *expressionistic*, symbolic form, the *slice-of-life story* portrays a simple situation on the surface, but comments on universal issues in depth (Joyce, Hemingway and his iceberg theory). Later forms include the *factual short story* (blending factual reality and fictional creation – Capote, Mailer, Wolfe), the *absurd anti-story* (human existence seen as senseless – Dylan Thomas, Selby, Burroughs), or the *meta-story* (reality as non-existent). The last decades have also witnessed some changes of perspective, for example *women's stories*, *post-colonial stories*, and voices from various minorities.

Variety of teaching approaches

As there are a multitude of story types, teachers will have no problem finding suitable stories in the publishers' catalogues. They may choose a single story because it fits the topic just discussed in the textbook, the time of year or a current event. There is also the longer way of reading several stories linked by a certain idea, and this approach offers something to appeal to everybody's tastes: author-based reading (e.g. Hemingway stories), nation-specific (e.g. Great American short stories), topic-based (e.g. post-colonial stories), genre-based (detective / fantasy / science fiction stories), gender-related (Women's stories) etc.

6.4 Storytelling

Can you imagine becoming a good story-teller?

Advantages of storytelling

Telling stories is a skill teachers should try to learn and develop – in particular when teaching younger learners. Children have an innate love of stories because they create magic, evoke a sense of wonder at the world, teach them about life, themselves and others. In the classroom, storytelling can enhance intercultural understanding, offer insights into universal life experiences, promote listening skills, encourage imagination and creativity, increase children's willingness to communicate thoughts and feelings, and promote a feeling of well-being.

Lessons about life

Listening to simple stories teaches children simple yet valuable lessons about life. *The Little Red Hen* (Michael Foreman, Red Fox, 1999) tells them that one must help people. In *The Very Hungry Caterpillar* (Eric Carle, Puffin Books, 1970) they get to know the life cycle of the butterfly. *Meerkat in Trouble* (Allan Frewin Jones, Happy Cat Books, 1998) points out the necessity of being obedient to one's parents. *The Pied Piper* (Eva Johannsen, Bremer Drucksachen Service, 2000) teaches them to keep their promises and not be greedy. In *Tusk Tusk* (David McKee, Red Fox, 1978) they learn about respect, tolerance and racism.

Becoming a storyteller

Not everybody is a born storyteller, but everybody can learn to do it, and practice makes perfect. The more you tell stories in your classroom, the better you will become at it, and the more your children – and you – will enjoy it. Master storytellers like Andrew Wright (1995) and Richard Martin (2000) have given us a lot of valuable advice on how to captivate an audience with the right techniques (also see Ellis/Brewster 2002, Klippel 2000).

The art of storytelling	
Selecting the story	• Stories the teacher also likes • Authentic children's literature • Great authors (Aiken, Briggs, Carle, Dahl, Hill, McGough, Rosen, Sendak, Dr. Seuss) • Various sources (big storybooks, anthologies, journals, newspapers, internet) • Structural and rhetorical devices (repetition, cumulative content, rhyme, onomatopoeia) • Humour and suspense • Illustrations synchronising with the text
Remembering the plot	• Use story skeletons for the key events • Think of the plot as a film (a series of connected images) • Tell yourself the story in your own words • Adapt and improvise (create your own version) • Retell it numerous times (Wright: 5 times)
Starting the story	• Arouse curiosity and build up tension • Use a special seating arrangement (circle of chairs, sitting on the floor) • You may darken the room (blinds down) • Use non-verbal sign or bell as a signal to start • Make the first sentences captivating
Performance techniques	• Vary the volume, speed and pitch of your voice • Use your face, body and gestures (let your body speak) • Use different, exaggerated character voices • Have a clear focus • Be dynamic but do not move too much • Maintain engaging eye contact with the audience and individual listeners • Pace yourself depending on how the children are following you • Involve and interact with the children (answering, repeating, elaborating, TPR) • Use silence and pauses for dramatic effect
Post-storytelling outcome	• Dramatization • Book-making • Related songs and rhymes • Making a game (quiz, competition) • Poster-design • Project work etc.

Storytelling and storyreading

Storytelling usually means telling a story freely. Reading out a story from a book may be a good alternative for teachers who have little experience and feel awkward having to use a foreign language in an expressive and dramatic way. Moreover Storyreading takes less time in preparation, the text is always the same and without mistakes, there are illustrations in the book, and dramatic role reading can also be captivating. However, when reading, you tend to speak too fast, and it becomes more difficult to support the story with non-verbal means of communication, with the effect that you lose your children.

Tasks

1. Write a mini-saga.
2. What are the answers to the two linguistic puzzles?
3. Read Dorothy Parker's *You Were Perfectly Fine* and identify the six main features of a short story.
4. Choose a simple story and tell it out loud. Make use of the suggestions for preparation and presentation given in the table. You may want to use *The Little Red Hen*.

The Little Red Hen

One day as the Little Red Hen was scratching in a field, she found a grain of wheat.
"This wheat should be planted," she said. "Who will plant this grain of wheat?"
"Not I," said the Duck.
"Not I," said the Cat.
"Not I," said the Dog.
"Then I will," said the Little Red Hen. And she did.
Soon the wheat grew to be tall and yellow.
"The wheat is ripe," said the Little Red Hen. "Who will cut the wheat?"
"Not I," said the Duck.
"Not I," said the Cat.
"Not I," said the Dog.
"Then I will," said the Little Red Hen. And she did.
When the wheat was cut, the Little Red Hen said, "Who will thresh the wheat?"
"Not I," said the Duck.
"Not I,"said the Cat.
"Not I, " said the Dog.

"Then I will," said the Little Red Hen. And she did.
When the wheat was threshed, the Little Red Hen said, "Who will take this wheat to the mill?"
"Not I," said the Duck.
"Not I," said the Cat.
"Not I," said the Dog.
"Then I will," said the Little Red Hen. And she did.
She took the wheat to the mill and had it ground into flour.
Then she said, "Who will make this flour into bread?"
"Not I," said the Duck.
"Not I," said the Cat.
"Not I," said the Dog.
"Then I will," said the Little Red Hen. And she did.
She made and baked the bread. Then she said, "Who will eat this bread?"
"Oh! I will," said the Duck.
"And I will," said the Cat.
"And I will," said the Dog.
"No, No!" said the Little Red Hen. "I will do that." And she did.

www.bres.boothbay.k12.me.us/wq/nnash/WebQuest/little_red_hen.htm – 05/09/07

7 Novels

7.1 Classroom canon

What novels did you read at school?

Definition

The term *novel* covers a variety of writings that share the characteristics of being extended (> 50,000 words) fictitious prose narratives. It is a derivative from the Italian *novella*, i.e. a little new thing, yet today when we speak of a novella, we mean a short novel (20,000-50,000 words), e.g. Hemingway's *Old Man and the Sea*. Though the scope of different forms renders any attempt of pinning down its features futile, a novel usually shows people in significant action, so important elements are action and in particular the description of characters, how they discover things, grow, learn, develop – or alternatively don't develop.

Most popular novels

Turning to the classroom, the question arises as to which of the numerous novels are the most popular? A survey asking 400 students at Cologne University what novels they had read during their school years, produced the following Top Ten novels of German TEFL classrooms (Nünning 1997). (The last column indicates what percentage of the people asked had read this novel.)

Top Ten novels

Rank	*Author*	*Novel*	%
01	William Golding	Lord of the Flies	35
02	Aldous Huxley	Brave New World	34
03	George Orwell	Animal Farm	31
04	J.D. Salinger	The Catcher in the Rye	29
05	George Orwell	1984	20
06	Bernard MacLaverty	Cal	7,8
07	Scott Fitzgerald	The Great Gatsby	7,6
08	Ray Bradbury	Fahrenheit 451	7,1
09	John Steinbeck	The Pearl	5
10	Alan Sillitoe	The Loneliness of the Long Distance Runner	4

Problems

There is a strong focus on just a few titles: two thirds of the responses are concentrated on the top six novels. The actual variety of Anglo-American literature is not reflected at all in classroom reading. From an historical point of view, nine out of ten novels were published between 1910 and 1960, which means that contemporary novels are widely ignored (so are those from the 18th and 19th century). A geographical perspective shows that British authors take the lead, American writers cannot quite catch up, and novels from other parts of the English speaking world, e.g. New English literatures, do not seem to exist – in contrast to Nobel Prize and Booker Prize ceremonies which acknowledge multiculturalism, regional consciousness and the internationalisation of English literature (Naipaul, Coetzee – Rushdie, Ondaatje, Doyle, Atwood etc.). As for the gender of the authors, women writers are non-existent. To put it into a nutshell, classroom discussion of novels is dominated by the DWEM's (Dead White English Males).

Uniformity of canon

A comparison with a similar survey conducted 20 years earlier proves that hardly anything has changed. Six of the ten titles were also ranked in the 1976 survey, the top three in both studies were *Lord of the Flies*, *Brave New World* and *Animal Farm*. There is a strong uniformity in the canon, which has proved to be very resistant to change.

... and its reasons

The reasons for this phenomenon are not hard to identify. Without any doubt, the novels in the rankings are among the great works of English literature and deserve their status as classics. In addition, however, teachers also teach what they were taught, often resorting to the books they had read during their school or university years. Moreover a vicious circle involving teachers and publishers causes this overemphasis on a few titles: publishers concentrate their study aids and model analyses on the popular texts; teachers prefer those novels that come along with handy teaching material.

Opening the canon

The problem, however, is that a uniform and static canon does not represent the actual scope of English literature, excludes a great wealth of suitable novels, and ignores the needs and interests of present-day students, who no longer attend the classrooms of the 1950s. Furthermore reading authentic novels should not be confined to the advanced classes either, but may well start at intermediate level. An alternative Top Ten, which includes contemporary authors, women writers, postcolonial literature, postmodern writing, and also easy-to-read young adult novels or crime fiction, may look like this:

Alternative Top Ten

Rank	*Author*	*Novel*
01	Julian Barnes	England, England
02	Philip Roth	The Human Stain
03	Zadie Smith	White Teeth
04	Margaret Atwood	The Handmaid's Tale
05	Agatha Christie	And Then There Were None
06	Louis Sachar	Holes
07	Mark Haddon	The Curious Incident of the Dog in the Night-Time
08	Jonathan Safran Foer	Everything Is Illuminated
09	Chinua Achebe	Things Fall Apart
10	Lois Lowry	The Giver

7.2 Types of novels

What different types of novels do you know?

Variety of sub-genres

There are a lot of subgenres of novels, which makes the confinement of the classroom canon to dystopias and a few other types even more disheartening. A good overview of the various categories helps the teachers in their choice of suitable novels for their classes. Students also profit from genre awareness by increasing the scope of appropriate material for their private reading as well as their autonomy in selection. The following survey describes some of the genres relevant for our students.

Types of novels

Type	*Description*	*Examples*
Apologue	A moral fable, usually featuring personified animals or inanimate objects acting like people, allowing the author to comment on humankind	George Orwell: *Animal Farm*, Rudyard Kipling: *The Jungle Book*
Autobiographical novel	A novel based on the author's life experience	James Joyce: *Portrait of the Artist as a Young Man*, Frank McCourt: *Angela's Ashes*

Coming-of-age story	A type of novel where the protagonist is initiated into adulthood, often by a process of disillusionment	Jane Austen: *Northanger Abbey*, J.D. Salinger: *The Catcher in the Rye*
Detective novel	A novel focusing on the solving of a crime, often by a brilliant detective, usually employing the elements of mystery and suspense	Sir Arthur Conan Doyle: *The Hound of the Baskervilles*, Agatha Christie: *And Then There Were None*
Chick lit	Fiction marketed to young women, especially single, working women in their 20s and 30s, in urban settings, following their love lives and struggles in business	Helen Fielding: *Bridget Jones's Diary*, Candace Bushnell: *Sex and the City*
Dystopian novel	An anti-utopian novel where everything has gone wrong in the attempt to create a perfect society	Aldous Huxley: *Brave New World*, Lois Lowry: *The Giver*
Fantasy novel	A novel that is disengaged from reality, often set in nonexistent worlds, such as under the earth, in a fairyland, etc.	J. R. R. Tolkien: *The Hobbit*, Joanne Rowling: *Harry Potter*
Hypertext novel (hyperfiction)	A novel that can be read in a non-sequential way, one can move from one place in the text to another whenever one wishes to trace an idea or follow a character	Michael Joyce: *Afternoon*, Stuart Moulthrop: *Victory Garden*
Interactive novel	A novel with more than one possible series of events or outcomes, at various places the reader can choose what will happen next	Geoff Ryman: *253 – or Tube Theatre*, Rob Swigart: *Portal*
Lad lit	The male equivalent to chick lit, focusing on young men in their 20s and 30s	Nick Hornby: *About a Boy*, Tony Parsons: *Man and Boy*
Multicultural novel	A novel written by a member of or about a cultural minority group, giving insight into non-western cultural values	Alice Walker: *The Color Purple*, Zadie Smith: *White Teeth*
Pulp fiction	Novels written for the mass market, intended to be "a good read", often exciting, titillating, thrilling	dime novels, Westerns, stories of adventure, Horatio Alger novels

Science fiction novel	A novel in which futuristic technology or scientific principles contribute in a significant way to the adventures	H. G. Wells: *The Invisible Man*, Arthur Clarke: *2001: A Space Odyssey*
Utopian novel	A novel that presents an ideal society where the problems of poverty, greed, crime etc. have been eliminated	Thomas More: *Utopia*, Samuel Butler: *Erewhon*
Young adult novel	A novel written for or marketed to young adults, mostly centred around a young adult protagonist	Lois Lowry: *The Giver*, Luis Sachar: *Holes*

Young adult novels

Although all genres contain suitable reading material for our students, the last type in particular seems suitable for them. It is not only that young adult novels are published for young people roughly between 12 and 18, portray an adolescent as the protagonist, and have story-lines and subject matters which are consistent with the experience of the addressees. They are also often written in relatively simple language, so that they can be read with intermediate classes as well. Teachers, of course, are asked to choose appropriate titles. Many of them have *edgy* content, i.e. the situations depicted and social issues addressed may be on the edge of what is considered acceptable. Whether the fictional portrayal of teens confronted with difficult situations (crime, violence, sexuality, drugs etc.) encourages destructive and immoral behavior, or instead helps readers deal with real-life challenges, is a disputed matter.

Blurred boundaries

Distinctions between type or genre are useful descriptive devices, but critics often regard them as rather arbitrary ones. In recent times genre boundaries have been subject to flux and blur, and a successful novel today frequently combines different types in some original way.

7.3 Reading approaches

Should the students have read the whole novel before it is discussed in class?

6 approaches to reading novels

As the novel is an extended piece of fiction it cannot be read in one lesson. So the question arises as to what the best approach to reading looks like. There are basically six approaches, which are summarised in the following table.

Reading a novel	
Approach	*Description*
Straight Through Approach	The whole novel is read at home by the students before classroom discussion starts.
Segment Approach	In each lesson one segment (or chapter) is discussed in class. This may be prepared at home or/and read at school.
Sandwich Approach	Some chapters of the novel are read, others are skipped.
Appetizer Approach	Only one excerpt from the whole book is read and discussed.
Topic Approach	Several books from the same literary genre, period, author or on a single issue are read in excerpts.
Patchwork Approach	Several books from various authors, genres and periods are read (in excerpts) and discussed.

Straight through approach

The *straight through approach* requires that all students have read the whole novel before starting work in class, which poses a problem for lazy readers. They may get around this assignment by asking schoolmates for a quick briefing or by skimming a short plot summary on the Web. Another drawback may be that being informed about the outcome of the story decreases interest and tension. Some of the benfits of this approach, however, are that knowing the whole story eases understanding, topic-oriented explorations can be based on the full text, and all of the classroom time can be spent on discussion and analysis.

Segment approach

The *segment approach* still covers the whole of the novel, keeps the suspense of the story, does not expect too much reading of the students per day, and lends itself to a combination of pre-, while- and post-reading activities. Some readers may object to cutting up a text into easily digestible bits, enforcing a uniform pace of reading. Moreover this approach is quite time-consuming.

Sandwich approach

Less time is needed for the *sandwich approach*, which leaves out parts of the story that are not so important, providing the missing information in varied forms (short presentations by teacher or students, gapped summaries, questions for intelligent guessing, true/false statements etc.). The students' attention is focused on the key passages. Readers who are interested may catch up on reading the pages skipped in class at home. Those who do not (because they do not have to), however, may face problems of understanding if longer passages are left out. Such a broken-up reading process causes them to get a distorted impression of the book.

Appetizer approach

Least time is taken up by the *appetizer approach*. Teachers feel free to choose a passage, focus on some important theme or technique, and intensify understanding by repeated reading and detailed analysis questions. Isolating one key segment, of course, ignores much of the context, cannot provide a profound understanding of what a novel is about, and may leave the learners with a feeling of frustration. Their appetite being whetted, they may embark on reading the whole text, though.

Topic approach

The *topic approach* may focus on an author (e.g. Joanne Rowling), a literary genre (e.g. dystopias), period (e.g. 21st century novels) or a certain social, cultural, political issue (e.g. the role of women). Reading various excerpts on one and the same topic can deepen understanding, yet an appreciation of the nature of the whole novel cannot be achieved in this way.

Patchwork approach

This qualification is also true for the *patchwork approach*, which samples the delights of reading novels by picking bits and pieces from various writers, times and types. This procedure may well be suited for a literary history en miniature unit, which includes factual information on the socio-cultural background of the various periods.

Teaching Unit: segment approach

The segment approach has been chosen for the following unit lesson plan, which is based on Mark Haddon's award-winning novel *The Curious Incident of the Dog in the Night-time*. This moving book is centred around a boy named Christopher, who happens to be suffering from Asperger's syndrome, a form of autism. The reader follows him as he tries to find the murderer of his neighbor's dog, Wellington. While looking for the murderer, Christopher decides to write a murder mystery novel, which is what we are supposed to be reading. The unit plan, prepared by Patrice Flood for first language learners but adaptable for TEFL classrooms, includes lots of different media and activities (articles, technology, music, art, films, poetry, performance) in order to appeal to various learner types. Students are expected to read a segment of the novel for each lesson and keep a journal of their readings.

Teaching Unit	
Topic:	*The Curious Incident of the Dog in the Night-Time*
Aims:	extensive reading, keeping a reading journal, intertextual and intermedial awareness
Level:	from grade 9
Time:	10 lessons
Procedure:	Lesson 1: information on Asperger's Syndrome and autism (pre-reading activity) – homework: read up to p. 32 Lesson 2: facial expressions – homework: read up to p. 61 Lesson 3: comparison with first chapter of *The Hound of the Baskervilles* – homework: read up to p. 102 Lesson 4: similes, metaphors, and signs – homework: read up to p. 140 Lesson 5: creative writing (The land of Aspergia) – homework: read up to p. 177 Lesson 6: comparing poems – homework: read up to p. 198 Lesson 7: WebQuest – homework: read up to the end Lesson 8: watching *Rain Man* – homework: choose a scene to act out Lesson 9: practising the scenes for performance Lesson 10: performance – homework: write a *critical lens* essay
Materials:	novel, handouts, supplementary material (DVD etc.)

7.4 Exploiting techniques

How can we make full and effective use of the different elements of a novel?

Analysing a novel

Apart from reading, literary communicative competence (LCC) also comprises the skills of understanding and creating. So after choosing an appropriate reading approach, suitable procedures have to be employed to exploit the various dimensions of a novel and improve the students' narrative competence. As far as analysis and interpretation are concerned, the following aspects deserve closer inspection:

Analysing a novel	
Composition	• story vs discourse • levels of communication: real author/reader, fictive narrator/reader, characters • genre
Point of view	• 1st/3rd person • omniscient/limited • reliable/unreliable • overt/covert narrator • multiperspectivity
Characters	• protagonist/antagonist/foil • characterization: explicit/implicit, by narrator/another character, self/others
Plot	• story vs plot • types: initiation, quest, courtship • beginning: ab ovo, in medias res • ending: closed, deus ex machina, open, happy, tragic
Setting	• time: – order (chronological, anachronic: flashback, flash-forward) – duration (discourse time, story time, scene, summary, stretch) – frequency (singulative, repeating, iterative) • place: represented by narrator/character, semanticisation
Style	• usage • diction • register • tone • rhetorical devices

Relevance of exposition

A lot of these devices can already be identified when reading the beginning of a novel, the exposition, or the first chapter. The exposition sets the action going, suggests the theme, introduces the main characters, sketches the setting, and arouses suspense. Therefore the analysis of a novel has to pay special attention to the beginning. It is also the favourite segment for an appetizer approach (7.3), and an aid in the process of selecting a novel, e. g. the first page of several novels can be handed out to the students to help them pick the one which they like best.

Example: Adrian Mole's Secret Diary

The following excerpt is the first chapter of Sue Townsend's cult novel *The Secret Diary of Adrian Mole Aged 13¾*, which is an unabashed glimpse into the troubled life of an acne-plagued adolescent. The genre is made clear (diary form of novel), the main characters are mentioned (a thirteen-year-old boy and his parents), the action is set going (Adrian reports his thoughts and experiences in his secret diary every day), the setting is implied (living together with Mum and Dad), the themes are indicated (the problems of growing up), suspense is aroused (secret diary as the form par excellence for presenting a youngster's intimate confessions), the point of view is established (1st person, limited), the relation to the reader is built up (reader as peeping Tom), the author's style is developed (mixture of tragedy and comedy, resulting from the contrast between earnest themes and lighthearted presentation).

Sue Townsend: ***The Secret Diary of Adrian Mole aged 13 ¾***

Chapter One
Thursday January 1st
BANK HOLIDAY IN ENGLAND,
IRELAND, SCOTLAND AND WALES

These are my New Year's resolutions:

1. I will help the blind across the road.
2. I will hang my trousers up.
3. I will put the sleeves back on my records.
4. I will not start smoking.
5. I will stop squeezing my spots.
6. I will be kind to the dog.
7. I will help the poor and ignorant.
8. After hearing the disgusting noises from downstairs last night, I have also vowed never to drink alcohol.

My father got the dog drunk on cherry brandy at the party last night. If the RSPCA hear about it he could get done. Eight days have gone by since Christmas Day but my mother still hasn't worn the green lurex apron I bought her for Christmas! She will get bathcubes next year.
Just my luck, I've got a spot on my chin for the first day of the New Year!

Creative pre-tasks

When trying to exploit a novel, the cognitive and analytical perspective should be complemented by creative, learner-centred, product or process-oriented activities. Before students start reading the novel, they may, among other things, be asked to predict from the title, the first or last lines, a key word or some visuals.

While-reading tasks

The reading process can be interrupted at convenient places to integrate various creative tasks. Transforming activities such as changing the point of view, replacing one character by another, or altering the setting, raise the students' awareness of the author's literary techniques. A narrative segment can also be transformed into a dialogue. Empathy is raised when students have to create *inside views* (thought bubbles). Personal involvement can also be fostered by asking them to keep a reading journal, in which they write down their personal responses to the story.

Post-reading tasks

After the last chapter, comprehension may be checked by activities such as answering questions, ticking off true-false statements, reordering sequences from the story, correcting a summary, unjumbling texts, or matching characters and quotations from the novel. Various follow-up tasks can round off the reading experience:

- writing a letter, a telegram, an agony aunt column, an epitaph, a book review, a newspaper article, the blurb
- discussing and debating controversial issues dealt with in the novel
- designing a promotional handout
- staging a press conference, a talk show, a panel discussion, *The Literary Quartet*
- interviewing the characters
- casting film stars to act the various characters
- dramatizing a segment of the story
- putting the author of the book on the *hot seat*
- creating a new character
- altering the end of the novel
- inventing another title

Tasks

1. Choose one novel and do the following tasks:
   a) (Re-) read it extensively.
   b) Write a three-sentence synopsis of this novel.

c) Justify in three sentences why it is a good read for TEFL classrooms.

2. The following table presents further types of novels. Unfortunately the entries in the three columns are in jumbled order. Put term (no.) and description (letter) into the right order again.

1. Adventure novel	a) A novel focusing on and describing in detail the social customs and habits of a particular social group (Austen: *Pride and Prejudice*)
2. Epistolary novel	b) A novel faithful to a particular geographic region and its people (Lee: *To Kill a Mockingbird*)
3. Gothic novel	c) An episodic, often autobiographical novel about a rogue or picaro (a person of low social status) wandering around and living off his wits (Fielding: *Jonathan Wild*)
4. Historical novel	d) A novel whose driving characteristic is the element of suspense or mystery, with strange, unexplained events, vague threats or terrors, unknown forces or antagonists (Poe: *The Murders in the Rue Morgue*)
5. Mystery novel	e) Several novels related to each other, by plot, setting, character, or all three. Book marketers like to refer to multi-volume novels as sagas (Lewis: *The Chronicles of Narnia*)
6. Novel of manners	f) An extended fictional prose narrative about improbable events involving uncommon characters, e.g. knights on a quest for a magic sword, fairies, trolls (King Arthur tales)
7. Picaresque novel	g) A novel consisting of letters written by a character or several characters (Richardson: *Pamela*)
8. Regional novel	h) A novel in which supernatural horrors and an atmosphere of unknown terror pervades the action. The setting is often a dark, mysterious castle, where ghosts and sinister humans roam menacingly (Shelley: *Frankenstein*)

9. Romance	i) A novel set in the western United States featuring the experiences of cowboys and frontiersmen (Wister: *The Virginian*)
10. Sentimental novel	j) A novel whose main theme is adventure, an exciting undertaking involving risk and physical danger, as its main theme (Stevenson: *Treasure Island*)
11. Series	k) A novel where fictional characters take part in actual historical events and interact with real people from the past (Scott: *Ivanhoe*)
12. Western	l) A type of novel, popular in the 18th century, that overemphasizes emotion and seeks to create emotional responses in the reader, with an overly optimistic view of human nature (Sterne: *Sentimental Journey*)

3. The following guide tells you how to write a characterization. Fill in the ten gaps.

How to write a characterization

1) Study the .... or relevant passage(s).
2) Highlight the .... that contain information about your character.
3) Draw a .... which contains basic dimensions of character and distinguishable parts of the text.
4) Fill in the grid guided by the dimensions of character (appearance, gender, age, religion, marital status, e.........., occupation, financial status, social status, hobbies, emotions, motivations, practices, fears, back-story) and using the highlighted passages.
5) Ask yourself the following questions:
   - Is she/he a main character (protagonist, hero, heroine), intermediate character or background character?
   - Does the character remain stable in the process of the story (static character) or does he change (.......... character)?
   - Is he defined by a single quality (flat character, type) or is he a complex individual (.......... character)?
6) Write your characterization, structuring it into introduction, body and ....
7) Do not just list the various features, but show their ....
8) Prove your statements by referring to and .... from the text.

9) After finishing, read your characterization.
10) Check on ...., content, and whether the various dimensions are included.

---

4. Read chapter 1 from Townsend's *The Secret Diary of Adrian Mole aged 13 ¾* again. What student-activating tasks would you use in the pre-reading stage?

5. Some of the more difficult literary terms (table in 7.4) are defined here. Put the following names into the proper places:

in medias res, covert narrator, register, diction, unreliable narrator, foil, story time, stretch, discourse, plot, repetitive mode, deus ex machina, iterative mode

a) a character who represents characteristics and values which are diametrically opposed to those of another character, usually the protagonist.
b) a writer's choice of words (formal or informal, abstract or concrete)
c) a style which is appropriate to a certain situation (scientific, commercial, legal, theological, psychological)
d) reflecting the causal links between the different events of the story
e) the actual period of time when the events of the story 'witnessed' by the reader take place
f) time suspension, time has a stop, story time is shorter than narrating time
g) telling once what happened several times.
h) telling several times what happened once
i) here: referring to all the manipulations of the story that normally occur in a narrative, all the material an author adds to a story
j) the convention of beginning 'in the middle of things', rather than at the very start of the story
k) a narrator who neither refers to him/herself nor addresses any narratees, one who has a neutral (nondistinctive) voice
l) a narrator who gives his/her own interpretation of a story, instead of the author's (see Henry James)

m) some improbable, unexpected, artificial device, character or event which is suddenly introduced to resolve a situation (e.g. the impoverished hero is saved by an unexpected inheritance)

8 Poetry

8.1 Definition and status

Can you understand why pupils – and teachers – do not like poetry in the classroom?

Characteristics and benefits

Children have a natural affinity for poetry beginning with their first exposure to nursery rhymes and stories with repetitive lines. In preschool and kindergarten the children often sit down in a circle and recite finger plays and seasonal chants. It is no wonder then that most of us intuitively recognize a poem. Yet it is hard for us to give an exact definition of poetry. Normative definitions of what a poem is often refer to a single characteristic, with the risk of ignoring the multitude of different forms of poetry. Descriptive definitions, which list several criteria, follow a more pragmatic approach. The following grid combines a descriptive definition based on Müller-Zettelmann's multi-component model (2000) with the resulting implications and benefits for teaching poetry in the English language classroom.

Features of poetry		**Benefits for teaching**
Brevity		• Flexible use (various goals, all levels) • Use in one lesson • Use in lower grades
Density of subject matter (reduction, compression)		• Close reading required • Focus on essentials • Intensive reception
Increased subjectivity (individual experience)	⇒	• Emotional loading • Personal reader's response • Intercultural learning
Musicality (proximity to songs)		• Nice listening experience • Activation of different senses • Easy to remember • Recitation • Songs as material
Aesthetic self-referentiality (self-reflexivity, artificiality)		• Personal appeal • extraordinariness

Structural complexity (lines, metre, stanza) Phonological complexity (sounds, rhyme) Morphological complexity (words, word formation) Syntactic complexity (arrangement of sentences) Semantic complexity (figurative language)	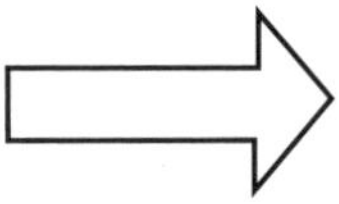	• Language awareness • Linguistic exploitability • Ambiguity • Interpretational openness • Stylistic analysis • Model for creative activities

Poetry boom

As one can see from the grid, making use of poetry in the language classroom can be beneficial in many ways. In addition, poetry as a literary form has experienced a renaissance in the last decades, at least in Great Britain and the USA. The famous project *Poetry on the Underground* on the London Tube, poetry slams in pubs, numerous forms of nonsense poetry in advertising as well as the book offers and sales figures of publishing companies testify to a new boom in the popularity of poetry – one of the reasons may be "dass nach Jahren seelenloser Profitgier der 80er Jahre nun eine neue Kultur des (Mit-)Fühlens angesagt sei" (Volkmann 1998: 5).

Cinderella existence in classrooms

In classrooms, however, poetry still seems to lead a Cinderella existence. Due to its complexity on different levels, poems in general are regarded by pupils as very hard to understand. If this is true for poems in the mother tongue, how much more difficult must poems written in a foreign language seem to be? Furthermore the increased self-referentiality of poems may mean that they are too far away from reality and students' immediate and personal experiences. Thus a lot of teachers avoid integrating lyric texts into their lessons as they fear a loss of motivation on the students' side. Unfortunately a one-sided teaching approach focusing on formalistic and analytic interpretation has widened the gap between poem and pupil. Poetry has often been maligned by excessive analysis of the poem and too much emphasis on "finding the meaning". Pupils have been made to memorize poems as part of class activities, and single poems too abstract or not of interest to the child have been used in isolation.

Opening canon and methodology

To overcome these barriers at least two developments have to be intensified. First the canon of poetry should be opened up, i.e.

beside Shakespeare sonnets other types of poetry which are short, easy and appealing should be included (8.3). "Mit diesem zu "*poetries*" hin erweiterten Lyrikbegriff müsste es gelingen, die für SchülerInnen meist abschreckende Vorstellung von einem Gedicht als ehrfurchtsvoll zu bewunderndem hermeneutischen Mysterium abzubauen" (Taubenböck 2004: 5). Second teaching methodology must be opened up, i.e. personal, creative, experimental and fun responses to poems should complement the more cognitive approaches (8.2) – because, as Wallace Stevens put it, "the purpose of poetry is to contribute to man's happiness."

8.2 Teaching options

How would you structure a poetry lesson?

PWP approach

The simplest and most common way to structure a poetry lesson is to resort to the process model and divide the unit into a pre-reading, while-reading and post-reading stage. The following table summarizes some suggestions for each of the three stages.

Structuring a poetry lesson

Process stage	*Activities*
P R E	• Introduction to author • Explanation of communicative situation • Discussion of title • Creative writing • Using media
W H I L E	• Reading whole text • Reading incomplete text • Reading changed text
P O S T	• First response • General understanding • Detailed analysis • Integrating background information • Evaluation • Recitation • Creating

Pre-reading stage

In the *pre-reading stage*, the teacher may give some information about the author of the poem and introduce the communicative situation (Who is speaking to whom about what?). Looking at the title, the students may speculate about the contents, thus activating their world knowledge; such a brainstorming or rather heartstorming activity may be done with the help of an association star on the board, i.e. a circle with a lot of rays on which the learners' ideas are written down. They may even write their own poem or parts of it on the title given. Different auditory or visual media (noises, pictures, photos, drawings etc.) can also introduce the topic of the poem and raise the students' curiosity.

While-reading stage

The *while-reading stage* mainly consists of the reading of the poem. The full text can be read – a few times – by the teacher, a (good) student (if the text is not too difficult) or presented via modern media if available, e.g. a recorded audio reading on CD, the Internet or an old record. For example, The Poetry Archive (www.poetryarchive.org) is an online collection of recordings of poets reading their work, and you can enjoy listening, free of charge, to the voices of contemporary English-language poets and poets from the past. The teacher can also hand out an incomplete or changed text. Various techniques may be employed here:

- *jumbled lines*: The poem is cut into separate lines, and the students have to put the lines into what they think is the correct order.
- *alternatives*: Some words of the poem are given two or three alternatives, and the students have to choose the one they think fits best.
- *two in one*: Two different poems are mixed into one, and the students have to sort them out.
- *prose and poem*: A poem is set like a prose text, and the students have to put it back into its lyrical form.
- *gapped poem*: Some words are deleted (rhyming words, first or last words of the lines, a few verses, a whole stanza), and the students have to complete the poem with suitable words. With younger or weaker students, a list with the original words can be added.
- *nonsense version*: Some words of the poem are replaced by other words, and the students have to underline and correct them. This technique is very suitable for listening to pop song lyrics, e.g. the classical song *Imagine* by John Lennon.

John Lennon: **Imagine** (nonsense version + proper version)	
1. Imagine there's a heaven Seize it if you cry No help below us A brother's only sky Imagine all the people Leaving for today	Imagine there's no heaven It's easy if you try No hell below us Above us only sky Imagine all the people Living for today
2. Imagine there's no counties It isn't a heart to woo Nothing to kill a fly for And a religion too Imagine all the people Living like a beast You may say I'm a dreamboat But I'm not the lonely one I hope Sunday you'll enjoy us And the world will be this one	Imagine there's no country It isn't hard to do Nothing to kill or die for And no religion, too Imagine all the people Living life in peace You may say I'm a dreamer But I'm not the only one I hope some day you'll join us And the world will be as one
3. Imagine oh processions A wonder if you can No need for creed or anger A motherhood of man Imagine all the people Cheering all the word You may say ...	Imagine no possession I wonder if you can No need for greed or hunger A brotherhood of man Imagine all the people Sharing all the world

Working with nonsense versions

The benefits of working with all these distorted text versions result from the way it is like a puzzle. It is motivating to play the detective, find missing things, and reconstruct the order. During this process the learners get a feeling for formal and thematic features of poetry, and dig below the surface of the written words. The aim, however, is not for the students to find the exact wording of the original. There is no right or wrong, various linguistic alternatives are possible, sensible guesses are asked for, choices should be justified, so that the learners learn to really concentrate on a text und grasp its basic meaning. This may lead to a deeper analysis later on if necessary.

Post-reading stage

In the *post-reading stage* students should get the chance to express their personal reactions to what they have heard or read. Such an exchange and discussion of first impressions may be followed by a general comprehension stage. The type of poem is decided upon (narrative, descriptive, reflective?), the situation is explained if this has not been done before (Who is speaking? Whom is he addressing?), the subject matter is clarified (What is the main theme? What does the title have to do with the theme?), the main intention is discussed (What is the message? What response is he trying to evoke?), the tone is described (What is the prevailing mood?). A general understanding of the poem could lead on to a detailed analysis, in which the various poetic devices in the fields of structure, phonology, morphology, syntax and semantics are studied (8.4). Analysis in itself is not bad if it is done in moderation and the right spirit. It should be pursued insofar as it illuminates the poem for the readers on their appropriate level. Poetry should be offered up for students to find their own connection to it, if any.

Evaluation

For a satisfactory interpretation one should also study the background of the poem as regards its literary history and biographical context. Based on all those findings, a balanced personal evaluation of the poem may modify the first impressions expressed immediately after the reading phase.

Reciting a poem

As poems are made up of sounds and rhythm, they should also be read aloud and recited. This can be turned into a fun experience, deepen the understanding of the poem and make students aware that active readers impart their own meaning to a passage and this determines the effect on the listener. Recitation has to be prepared, of course; in small groups, and supported by the teacher, students have to reflect on metre, rhythm, pauses, stress, volume, mood, body language and other poetic constituents. Various forms of reciting can be made use of:

- *choral reading*: The whole class – or smaller groups – recite the poem.
- *role reading*: The poem is read with different roles (e.g. boys and girls take turns)
- *mood reading*: The tone or volume may be changed (e.g. happy vs angry, loud vs whispering)
- *chain reading*: Each student of the class reads one line only until the whole class has participated.
- *stop and go*: One student starts and stops whenever he/she likes. His/her neighbour has to go on.
- *commented reading*: A student reads out and from time to time inserts *asides*, i.e. says what he/she likes or does not understand.

Poe-try

The post-reading stage, however, should not solely consist of recitation and cognitive tasks. As follow-up or transfer, numerous creative activities can be employed. There are written forms (e.g. adding another stanza), visual forms (e.g. putting the poem into a collage), musical forms (e.g. combining the text with a suitable melody), audiovisual forms (e.g. producing a short video clip – and uploading it onto You Tube), interactive forms (making a contribution to one of the various poetry websites). Poetry also exists to play about with, to experiment with, to try out alternative ideas – because poetry may also be written *poe-try*.

Teaching Unit for younger pupils

The following teaching idea follows the pre – while – post approach, is aimed at younger pupils and may be of use in the primary classroom.

Teaching Unit	
Topic:	*I'm a Friendly Snowman*
Aims:	reading, listening, speaking, writing (integrated skills)
Level:	from grade 4
Time:	one 45-minute lesson
Procedure:	- pre-reading phase: - *snowman* transparency (OHP) – successive uncovering as guessing game OR - feeling box: snowman objects in a box (hat ...) – pupils feel – guess the topic - while-reading phase: riddle: the word *snowman* is changed to *who* – teacher reads out – pupils guess who *who* is - post-reading phase: - matching picture cards and poem lines - class chain: reading aloud one line – learning by heart - creative writing: I'm a Friendly Easter Bunny
Materials:	text of *I'm a Friendly Snowman* I'm a friendly snowman big and fat, Here is my tummy and here is my hat. I'm a happy fellow, here is my nose, I'm all snow from my head to my toes. I have two bright eyes so I can see, All the snow falling down on me. When the weather's bad, I'm strong and tall, But when it's warm, I get very small.

8.3 Types of poetry

Do you know what a haiku is? And a clerihew? What about spoonerisms?

Poetries "If it ain't fun, it ain't poetry" (Taubenböck 2004): If one takes this motto seriously, traditional forms of poetry like sonnets, ballads, odes or dramatic monologues have to be complemented by alternative types. The following diagram displays the wealth of poetic forms including some of the more innovative, unconventional forms – the singular form *poetry* could really be replaced by the plural *poetries*.

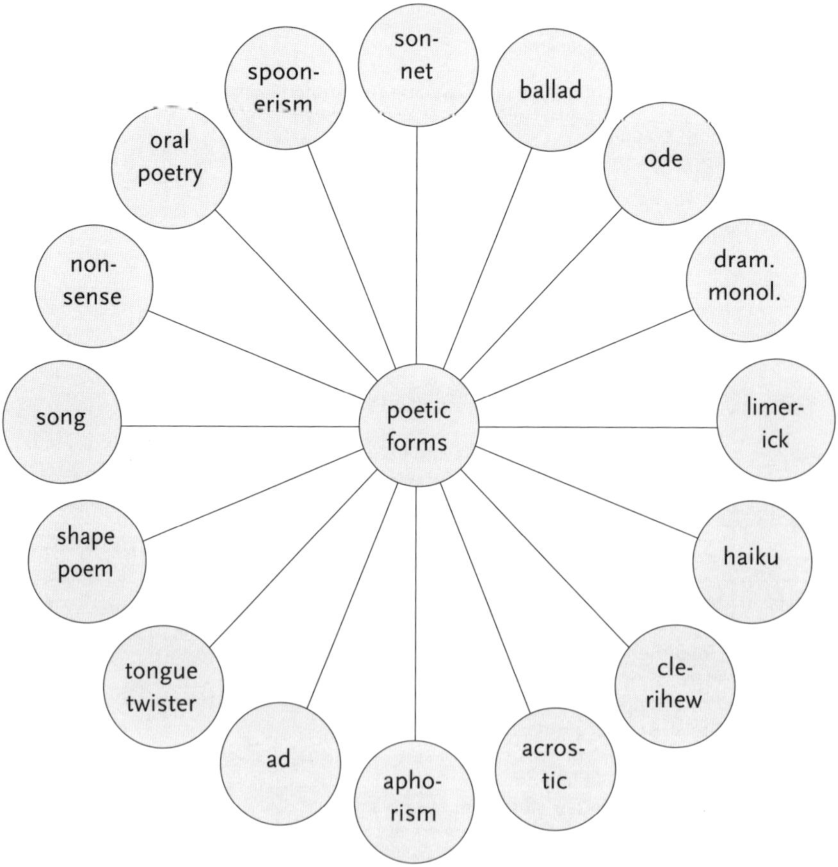

Short and sweet

In the following, some of the less traditional, shorter and more humorous types will be briefly described, together with some methodological ideas and an example to illustrate the genre.

Limericks

A *limerick* is a five-liner popularized by Edward Lear with a strict metre (the first, second, and fifth lines are three feet, the third and fourth are two feet). The rhyme scheme is usually aabba. The first line usually introduces a person and a location (at the end). A true limerick is supposed to have a kind of twist to it, which often lies in the final line. To introduce students to limericks, the teacher could first show them a few examples of this popular genre, followed by a short analysis of structure and form. Then one of the limericks may be presented in cloze form, with the students trying to fill in the gaps. After that just the structural form of another limerick is given, and the whole class create their poem. In a final step students in pairs or individually write their own limerick.

A limerick

A young man from the city of Poona,
Decided to fish from a schooner.
But he drank so much rum,
That it upset his tum,
So he didn't catch very much tuna.

Nonsense verse

Nonsense verse refers to poetry which is normally composed for humorous effect. The paradoxical, silly, witty, or just strange effect may result from nonsense words, i.e. words without a clear meaning or any meaning at all (Lewis Carroll, Edward Lear), incompatible word pairs that make grammatical sense but not a semantic one, ambiguous grammar, or nonsensical situations. Nonsense poetry has a long tradition, particularly in English, as it reflects the absurdist tendency in British humour. Such poems lend themselves to linguistic analysis, which aims at finding the source of the nonsense, or may simply be enjoyed for its whimsical appeal.

Two nonsense poems	
1. 'I see' said the blind man to the deaf woman as he picked up his hammer and saw.	2. Pussy cat, pussy cat, Where have you been? I've been to Britain To meet Mr Bean.

Acrostics

An *acrostic* (from Greek *akróstichon*, *ákros*: "extreme", and *stíchos*: "verse") is a poem in an alphabetic script, in which the first letter or word of each verse in the text spells out another message. An acrostic may serve as an introduction to a new topic (instead of a mind map), with the teacher writing the letters of the headword below each other, and the students completing the lines with their background knowledge. It may also be employed as a frame for personal associations.

Acrostic on LOVE

L et us never part
O r at least not so soon
V agabonds who do not care about
E ternity but live here and now.

Clerihews

A *clerihew* is a short biographical humorous verse invented by Edmund Clerihew Bentley in the first half of the 19th century. It consists of four lines of irregular length, the third and fourth lines usually being longer than the first two (comic effect). The rhyme scheme is aabb. The first line introduces the subject's name, the following three lines show him/her from an unusual and humorous point of view. After the students have become acquainted with this form, the teacher could give them the first and last line of a clerihew; when the students have filled in the middle, it may be interesting to see who is closest to the original.

Two clerihews	
1. Professor Albert Einstein Always drew a fine line Between positive and negative And what was purely relative.	2. What I like about Clive Is that he is no longer alive. There is a great deal to be said For being dead.

A *spoonerism* is a play on words in which corresponding consonants, vowels, or morphemes are switched. The name is derived from Reverend William Archibald Spooner (1844 – 1930), who became notoriously famous for his liking of it. When not used on purpose, spoonerisms are slips of the tongue, if used intentionally they are considered a form of pun. They are not to be confused with *malapropisms*, i.e. incorrect usages of a word by substituting a similar-sounding word with different meaning. One task for the students could be to put the spoonerism right, and moreover to speculate about the situation in which the statement was used.

Spoonerisms

Three spoonerisms
"You have hissed all my mystery lectures, and were caught fighting a liar."
"Mardon me padam, this pie is occupewed."
"Let us raise our glasses to the queer old Dean."

A *haiku* is a Japanese form of poetry. The traditional 'hokku' consists of 5, 7, 5 on (the Japanese word *on* roughly corresponds to an English syllable), combines two different phrases, with a distinct grammatical break, and focuses on nature and the place of humans in nature. Modern haiku poets consider any subject matter suitable, often use three lines of no more than 17 syllables in total – three lines of 2, 3, and 2 metrical feet, with a pause after the second or fifth – and use caesura to contrast or compare two situations. It can be quite challenging for students to identify the different concepts or phrases, contrasts and caesura. Once a clever idea is found, writing one's own haiku can be done quite fast. Presentations in class can give rise to controversial interpretations.

Haikus

Two haikus	
1. empty room: one swinging coat hanger measures the silence	2. quietly dozing under a clock without hands: the museum keeper

Shape poems

The terms *concrete poetry*, *shape poetry*, *pattern poetry* or *visual poetry* refer to poetry in which, beyond the conventional elements of meaning (words, rhyme, metre), the typographical arrangement of words conveys the intended effect, e.g. open space between words signifying a tennis net and a gap of communication in McGough's famous *40-love* poem. Given a few examples as models, students usually have no problems creating their own shape poems – a task which they do with enjoyment and often stunning results.

Roger McGough: **40-love**

middle	aged
couple	playing
ten	-nis
when	the
game	ends
and	they
go	home
the	net
will	still
be	be-
tween	them

Aphorisms

Aphorisms are short, witty statements or quotes. "Für ihre Verwendung im Englischunterricht sprechen folgende Konstituenten: Kürze, Prägnanz, Sentenzhaftigkeit, Überraschungseffekt, Aufforderungscharakter (Provokation), Rhetorik/Stilistik, Humor (Ironie, Satire)" (Thaler 2004: 36). A list of 25 different techniques which may be used in working with aphorisms on all topics can be found in Thaler (2004).

Aphorism: topic	*Aphorism: example*
Politics	In politics if you want anything said, ask a man. If you want anything done, ask a woman. (M. Thatcher)
Man & Woman	A man in love is incomplete until he is married. Then he is finished. (Z.Z. Gabor)
School & Education	He who can, does. He who cannot, teaches. (G.B. Shaw)
Language	Language is the dress of thought. (S. Johnson)

Life & Meaning	In this world there are only two tragedies. One is not getting what one wants, and the other is getting it. (O. Wilde)

Misspelt poems

If you put spelling mistakes into a lyric text on purpose, the result is a *misspelt poem*. The obvious task here is to ask students to edit the text and write an orthographically correct version. Afterwards the discrepancy between English spelling and pronunciation as well as the issue of a spelling reform could be discussed.

Spelling chequer

Eye halve a spelling chequer
It came with my pea sea
It plainly marques four my revue
Miss steaks eye kin knot sea.

Eye strike a key and type a word
And weight four it two say
Weather eye am wrong oar write
It shows me strait a weigh.

As soon as a mist ache is maid
It nose be fore two long
And eye can put the error rite
Its rare lea ever wrong.

Eye have run this poem threw it
I am shore your pleased two no
Its letter perfect all the weigh
My chequer tolled me sew.

Pop song lyrics

Pop songs including *raps* are a very popular medium with children and teenagers (see 11.2). If Shakespeare lived today he might write song lyrics – and if Bob Dylan or Sting had lived in the Elizabethan age, they might have written sonnets. There are some wonderful examples of pop lyrics around, which may be enjoyed and exploited for linguistic and intercultural purposes. Sting's *I'm an Englishman in New York* may, apart from being subjected to poetic and cultural analysis, be compared to the short story *Jolly Corner* by Henry James (Thaler 2005).

Sting: **I'm an Englishman in New York**

I don't drink coffee I take tea my dear
I like my toast done on one side
And you can hear it in my accent when I talk
I'm an Englishman in New York

See me walking down Fifth Avenue
A walking cane here at my side
I take it everywhere I walk
I'm an Englishman in New York

I'm an alien I'm a legal alien
I'm an Englishman in New York
I'm an alien I'm a legal alien
I'm an Englishman in New York

Modesty, propriety can lead to notoriety
You could end up as the only one
Gentleness, sobriety are rare in this society
At night a candle's brighter than the sun

I'm an alien I'm a legal alien I'm an Englishman in New York I'm an alien I'm a legal alien I'm an Englishman in New York If "Manners maketh man" as someone said Then he's the hero of the day It takes a man to suffer ignorance and smile Be yourself no matter what they say	Takes more than combat gear to make a man Takes more than a license for a gun Confront your enemies, avoid them when you can A gentleman will walk but never run If "Manners maketh man" as ... I'm an alien ...

Epitaphs

Even religious texts may find their way into the classroom, such as *prayers* or *epitaphs*. An epitaph is a text, traditionally in verse, which honours the deceased, and is inscribed on a tombstone or plaque. A lot of poets have composed their own epitaphs prior to their death. A good epitaph is regarded to be one that is memorable, or makes one think, often addressing the readers and warning them about their own mortality. Some of them are even humorous, resorting to puns and other stylistic devices. All these features may be exploited in a classroom discussion.

Four epitaphs

- *Excuse my dust. (Dorothy Parker's proposed epitaph)*
- *I told you I was sick.*
- *He died in peace – his wife died first.*
- *Here lies Johnny Yeast. Pardon me for not rising.*

Counting-out rhymes

A *counting-out rhyme* is used in real life, as the name suggests, to count out people and determine the members of a team in a game. In younger classes, such rhymes can be spoken in small groups and acted out accordingly. When the counting is done several times, each player pupil has to say a different line, and the words really get stuck in their heads.

A counting-out rhyme

A man walked into a beer bottle shop
And asked for a bottle of beer.
Where's your money?
In my pocket.

Where's your pocket?
I forgot it.
Please step out.

Performing poems

Such a counting-out rhyme is a special case of *performing poems*, in which the speakers perform an action. As they combine verbal skills with bodily movements, these poems are predestined for the TPR approach (Total Physical Response). Students have to carry out what is asked of them, which tends to intensify the learning process. Moreover they learn how to use their voices effectively.

This is the way ...*: performing poem*

This is the way you brush your teeth, brush your teeth, brush your teeth.
This is the way you wash your hands, wash your hands, wash your hands.
This is the way you comb your hair, comb your hair, comb your hair ...

Performance poetry

Performing poems may be regarded as the stepping-stone to *performance poetry*, i.e. a form of oral poetry that is not written for print distribution, but specifically composed either for or even during performance before an audience (in pubs or at festivals). Whereas poetry readings feature poets reading their printed books for a live audience, performance poets use a different style suited for their oral presentations. Teachers may encourage their classes to prepare and organize their own poetry slams in class or public places.

8.4 Poetic devices

Do you think it is necessary to teach stylistic devices in class?

Various levels and text types

Poetic devices can be found on the levels of structure, phonology, morphology, syntax and semantics. Such stylistic devices also turn up in narrative and dramatic texts, which underlines the necessity of making students familiar with them.

Structural level

A structural analysis will look at the external structure of a poem, its internal structure, its metric pattern and its rhythm. The external structure is mainly based on its stanzaic form, i.e. how many lines of verse a stanza (*Strophe*) comprises (couplet: paired lines of verse, tercet: three lines, quatrain: four lines, pentameter: five lines, hexameter: six lines). Thematic and formal relations as well as breaks (thematic, spatial, temporal changes) within a poem determine its internal structure. An analysis of the metre, i.e. the regular pattern of stressed and unstressed syllables within a line of a poem, is called *scansion* or *scanning*. To scan a line involves finding out the kind of foot (smallest unit of verse: *Versfuß*) and the number of feet (tetrameter: four beats, pentameter: five beats, etc.) – plus marking the pauses and missing syllables, and determining the rhyme-scheme and the stanza form. The rhythm of a poem results from its metre, the length of the syllables, repetitions and the meaning of words. The following table lists some of the most important structural devices.

Structural devices

Term	*Explanation*	*Example*
Anapest	Foot: – – '–	with the greatest of ease
Blank verse	Poetry with a regular metre, but no rhyme	You stars that reign'd at my nativity, Whose influence hath alloted death and hell (Christopher Marlowe, Doctor Faustus)
Dactyl	Foot: '– – –	Just for a handful of silver he left us
Enjambement	Run-on line (*Zeilensprung*)	(1st line) My heart aches, and a drowsy numbness pains (2nd line) My sense, as though of hemlock I had drunk (Keats: *Ode to a Nightingale*)
Free verse	Poetry without regular metre or rhyme	All truths wait in all things They neither hasten their own delivery nor resist it, They do not need the obstetric forceps of the surgeon. (Walt Whitman, *Leaves of Grass*)

Heroic couplet	A pair of two verses in pair rhyme and iambic pentameter	So long as men can breathe, or eyes can see, So long lives this, and this gives life to thee. (Shakespeare: Sonnet 18)
Iamb	Foot: – '–	the dust of snow
Trochee	Foot: '– –	tiger, tiger, burning bright

Phonological level

On the phonological level the most important feature is rhyme, which generally means that two or more words sound the same from the last stressed vowel. Identifying the rhyme scheme and other phonological characteristics can help to understand and interpret a poem better because rhymes can structure the text, emphasize relationships and contrasts, and support thematic aspects. The following table lists some of the most common phonological figures.

Phonological devices

Term	*Explanation*	*Example*
Alliteration	Repetition of a sound at the beginning of neighbouring words	Peter Piper picked a peck of pickled peppers.
Alternate rhyme	*Kreuzreim (alternierender Reim)*	abab cdcd
Assonance	Repetition of internal vowel sounds in neighbouring words that do not end the same (vowel rhyme)	When I get shocked at the hospital by the doctor when I'm not cooperating (Eminem)
Consonance	Repetition of consonant sounds at the end of neighbouring words with different vowel sounds	'Out of this house' – said rider to reader (W.H. Auden)
Embracing rhyme	*Umarmender (umschlingender) Reim*	abba cddc
End rhyme	Rhyme at the end of lines	Tyger! Tyger burning bright In the forests of the night (William Blake: The Tyger)
Eye rhyme	Spelling suggests rhyme, but pronunciation is different	flow – how

Internal rhyme	*Binnenreim*	letters of joy from girl and boy
Onomatopoeia	Using words which imitate the sound they refer to (*Lautmalerei*)	The cuckoo whizzed past the buzzing bees.
Rhyming couplets	*Paarreim*	aa bb cc

Morpho-syntactical level

The form and effect of a poem is also determined by rhetorical figures on the morphological (words, word formation) and syntactic (sentence structure) level. Such figures, together with structural and phonological ones, contribute a lot to the coherence of a poem, which is all the more necessary as poems usually have little to offer in terms of plot and characters. Moreover they emphasize certain elements of the content and thus help "to establish relations of correspondence and opposition" (Ludwig 1994: 135). As it is not always easy to draw a line between morphological and syntactic features, the following table summarizes some important morpho-syntactic figures.

Morpho-syntactic figures

Term	*Explanation*	*Example*
Accumulation	Enumeration; a row of similar expressions	I have dared to love you wildly, passionately, devotedly, hopelessly. (Oscar Wilde)
Anaphora	Successive clauses (sentences) starting with the same word	Mad world! Mad kings! Mad composition! (Shakespeare, King John)
Antithesis	Contrast; opposing words, phrases, structures, characters, views	It's easier for a father to have children than for children to have a real father. (Alexander Pope)
Chiasmus	Reversal in the order of words in the two halves of a sentence (*Kreuzstellung*)	Love's fire heats water, water cools not love. (Shakespeare)
Ellipsis	Leaving out essential grammatical items	And he to England shall along with you. (Shakespeare, Hamlet)
Parallelism	Repeating similar or identical words, phrases, constructions in neighbouring lines, sentences, paragraphs	If I am occasionally a little overdressed, I make up for it by being always immensely overeducated. (Oscar Wilde)

Repetition	Deliberately using a word or phrase more than once	Tomorrow and tomorrow and tomorrow, creeps in this petty pace from day to day (Shakespeare, Macbeth)
Rhetorical question	Question to which the answer is obvious	Don't we all love peace?

Finally there are rhetorical figures on the semantic level (meaning of words). Whereas in films you see visual images, imagery in poetry must rely on words, which convey a figurative meaning. The following table describes the omni-present metaphor and a few other common semantic figures.

Semantic level

Semantic figures

Term	*Explanation*	*Example*
Allusion	Indirect reference to a famous event, person or piece of literature	To meet one's Waterloo, the Scrooge Syndrome, the old man and the computer
Anti-climax	Opposite of climax; string of statements ending with the weakest	For God, for country, and for football.
Climax	Row of statements from the weakest to the strongest	Friends, Romans, countrymen! (Shakespeare, Julius Caesar)
Euphemism	Using polite expressions for sth. unpleasant	To pass away (to die), friendly fire (own army)
Hyperbole	Exaggeration; overstatement; making sth./sb. greater than they are	A momentary separation from anyone to whom one has just been introduced is almost unbearable. (Oscar Wilde)
Irony	Meaning the opposite of what you say	What a wonderful day it is! (when there's a thunderstorm)
Litotes	Understatement; making sth./ sb. less important than they are	The Queen was not amused.
Metaphor	Poetical comparison without *like* or *as*	Life's but a walking shadow. (Shakespeare, Macbeth)
Oxymoron	Combination of two seemingly contradictory terms (condensed paradox)	O hateful love! O loving hate!" (Shakespeare, *Romeo and Juliet*)

Paradox	Seeming impossible at first glance, but being true at second thoughts	Fair is foul, and foul is fair. (Shakespeare, Macbeth)
Personification	Presenting ideas, objects, animals as persons	Death pays all debts. (proverb) a smiling moon, a jovial sun
Pun	Play on words (using homophones or homonyms)	Seven days without water makes one weak.
Simile	Comparison using *like* or *as*	A woman without a man is like a fish without a bicycle. (Irina Dunn) Thick as a brick (Jethro Tull)
Symbol	Sth. concrete (object, character, event) standing for sth. abstract	dove (peace), Cupid (love), scales (justice), sceptre (royal power), horseshoe (luck)
Synecdoche	Using a part instead of the whole (pars pro toto)	Lend me your ears. (Shakespeare, Julius Caesar)
Tautology	Repetition of a single idea in different words, phrases, sentences	With malice toward none, with charity for all. (Abraham Lincoln)

Explaining the functions

When analysing a poem it is, however, not sufficient to just identify the type of rhetorical device used. To achieve a deeper understanding of the meaning of a text, one has to reflect on the function of a rhetorical figure, i.e. why it is used in this specific context. Form and function are inter-related. The most common functions or effects of rhetorical figures are:

- to emphasize a certain aspect (most common function!)
- to arouse the reader's interest / to catch the reader's attention
- to make the reader think (don't overuse this argument!)
- to criticize / satirize a situation / person / idea / event
- to produce a fine rhythm
- to create humour
- to amuse / entertain the reader
- to evoke funny / revealing associations
- to create a graphic mental image
- to make the passage vivid
- to surprise the reader

As functions also depend on the specific context in which a rhetorical device is placed, students must be warned against making over-generalizations, stating functions without thinking. To understand poetic devices is an important goal in teaching literature, but poetry lessons must not be reduced to a formal analysis. Playful and creative activities should complement the more cognitive ones.

Tasks

1. Prepare and carry out a debate on the necessity of teaching poetry. The motion is: *Poems should be banned from TEFL classes.* There should be at least two proposers and two opposers. Before the vote is finally taken, the motion is put to the floor, i.e. all members of the debating club can state their opinions.
2. Choose one of the poems in 8.3 and design a 45-minute lesson around it. Divide your lesson plan into a pre-, while- and post-reading stage. Make use of the information given in this chapter.
3. Study the following examples of poetry (8.3) and do the tasks:
   a) spoonerisms: Put the three examples right by correcting the switched words.
   b) acrostics: Write an acrostic on HATE.
   c) misspelt poems: Find the spelling mistakes and write a correct version.
4. Look at the song lyrics *I'm an Englishman in New York* by Sting and find one example each of the following poetic devices:
   a) repetition
   b) anaphora
   c) parallelism
   d) allusion
   e) internal rhyme
   f) ellipsis
   g) antithesis
5. Draw a scansion chart of the following limerick:
   There was a young girl, a sweet lamb,
   Who smiled as she entered a tram.
   After she had embarked
   The conductor remarked,
   "Your fare!" and she said, "Yes, I am!"

6. Types of poetry: In the following table the names and definitions of ten common types of poetry are out of order. Match the numbers with the right letters.

(1) Ballad	(a) a short poem ending in a witty turn of thought
(2) Descriptive poem	(b) a short rhythmical poem, derived from folk song, expressing the the speaker's feelings or mood
(3) Elegy	(c) a simple poem in short stanzas, which tells a popular story in verse
(4) Epic	(d) a poem which describes people, objects, situations, or experiences
(5) Epigram	(e) a poem which tells a story and has external action
(6) Lyric poem	(f) a poem in an elevated style which is often sung in celebration of a special event
(7) Narrative poem	(g) a poem in which the speaker comments on a situation, ponders on a thought, draws conclusions from events
(8) Ode	(h) a poem of 14 lines consisting of iambic pentameters
(9) Reflective poem	(i) a poem which celebrates – in the form of a narration – the achievements of a heroic personality of the past
(10) Sonnet	(j) a solemn poem which deals with death and personal loss

9 Plays

9.1 Long and short types

What dramas did you read at school?

Nature of drama

Drama has a dual nature, i.e. it incorporates literary and representational art. *Dramatic* texts, in contrast to narrative and poetic ones, are texts written to be acted out in front of an audience. Several actors slip into the roles of characters, perform an action on a stage and speak the written words. Apart from the verbal code, they have to make ample use of non-verbal means of communication. All these features of drama should be kept in mind when proposing suggestions for teaching drama.

Most popular dramas

Now what are the most popular dramas in our classrooms? A survey which asked 400 students at Cologne University what dramas they had read during their school years, produced the following Top Ten dramas of TEFL classrooms in Germany (Nünning 1998).

Top Ten dramas

Rank	*Author*	*Play*	%
01	W. Shakespeare	Macbeth	56,5
02	A. Miller	Death of a Salesman	41,4
03	J.B. Priestley	An Inspector Calls	12,1
04	W. Shakespeare	Romeo and Juliet	9,5
05	W. Shakespeare	Julius Caesar	7,4
06	H. Pinter	The Caretaker	7,1
06	W. Russell	Educating Rita	
08	W. Shakespeare	Hamlet	5,5
08	G.B. Shaw	Pygmalion	
10	O. Wilde	The Importance of Being Earnest	5,0
10	W. Shakespeare	The Merchant of Venice	

Uniformity and stability

The results resemble those about the most popular novels: The DWEM's, i.e. Dead White English (and Irish) Males rule our classrooms. And their dominance has not been questioned for decades, since a similar survey carried out nearly 20 years earlier had produced the same results. Only one title (Russell's *Educating Rita*) entered the charts as a newcomer, all the others had already been mentioned in the 1978 study – though Osborne's *Look back*

Opening up the canon

in Anger, Miller's *All my Sons*, Williams' *The Glass Menagerie*, and Wilder's *Our Town* had given up their Top 10 notches (Nünning 1998: 6).

The list demonstrates a preponderance of Shakespeare (which is based on curricular guidelines), whereas contemporary dramas, women writers and authors other than English and Irish (and American) are widely ignored. The uniformity and stability of this drama canon suggests that "Drama und Theater ehrwürdige bildungsbürgerliche Institutionen sind, die primär der Vergangenheit angehören und in England in Shakespeare nicht nur ihren Höhe-, sondern auch ihren Endpunkt erreicht haben" (Nünning 1998: 6). Therefore Nünning, in an attempt to open up the canon, recommends an alternative Top Ten for the future (Ib.: 8).

Alternative Top Ten dramas

Author: Play (Year)	*Synopsis*
1. Peter Shaffer: *Amadeus* (1979)	Mozart's life and death as a memory play
2. Caryl Churchill: *Top Girls* (1982)	Stories of unconventional women
3. Alan Ayckbourn: *Henceforward* (1981)	Psychological thriller about an anti-utopian society
4. Peter Nichols: *Passion Play* (1981)	Passion play on the conflict between sexuality and Christian moral attitudes
5. Joe Orton: *Loot* (1965)	Anarchical farce on homosexuality and bourgeois society
6. Agatha Christie: *The Mouse Trap* (1952)	The most popular detective play of all times
7. Simon Gray: *Quartermain's Terms* (1981)	Psychological drama on alienation and school
8. Edward Bond: *Lear* (1971)	Contemporary political perspective on King Lear
9. Tom Stoppard: *Rosencrantz and Guildenstern Are Dead* (1967)	What Shakespeare revealed about Hamlet
10. David Hare: *Skylight* (1995)	Generation and relationship conflicts in a three-character play

Short forms

Apart from overcoming historic, national, ethnic, geographical and gender restrictions, opening up the drama canon should also look at the category of length. Dramatic texts are not only full-length tragedies and comedies, but include shorter forms as well. Due to their brevity they easily fit into the lessons, children are used to them from their first year of learning as short dialogues and role plays are an integral part of coursebooks from the beginning, and staging short forms does not need too much time, effort and props. Short plays, which usually have few characters, deal with a single problem, occur in a single setting, and immediately confront the reader / audience with a critical situation *in medias res*, comprise a great variety of types, which are appropriate for TEFL (Rau 1999, Hallet/Hebel 2007).

- dialogue scene
- role play
- story reading
- key scenes of full-length plays
- playlet
- skit
- one-act play
- pantomime
- shadow show
- silhouette
- puppet show
- frozen tableau
- radio play
- film scenes
- sketch

Teaching Unit: *Dead Parrot*

Tribute for inventing the most famous sketch of the world is frequently paid to Monty Python and their legendary *Dead Parrot* (Flying Circus, Series 1, Show 9). In a pet shop, John Cleese is trying desperately to give back a dead parrot, but Michael Palin as the shopkeeper refuses because he seems determined that the parrot was already dead when he sold it. In particular the ingenuity on the linguistic level (dialogue structure, mixing different registers and sociolects, argumentation) has given this sketch cult status.

Teaching Unit	
Topic:	*Dead Parrot*
Aims:	viewing skills, analysing a sketch, linguistic awareness
Level:	from grade 10
Time:	one or two lessons
Procedure:	1. *Pre-viewing* – Have you ever had to complain about anything? Tell us. – Have you ever had to return a faulty thing? How did the shop-assistant react? 2. *While-viewing* – 1st viewing ▸ Describe the communicative situation: who, where, what, why, how. – Studying the annotations (transparency or hand-out) – 2nd viewing ▸ When did you laugh? Why? How does the customer try to convince the shopkeeper that the parrot is dead? How does the shopkeeper distract the customer? – 3rd viewing of end ▸ word field "to die": lexical memory game: Write down as many words for "to be dead" as you can remember. You have two minutes time. 3. *Post-viewing* role play: One pupil wants to exchange a faulty object (CD player, computer ...), the other tries to reject it. Work in pairs, write down the dialogue, and act it out. *Homework*: Write a sketch about your teacher and yourself. You try to talk your way out of having forgotten your homework. (If you forget your homework, you will have to perform the sketch in class.)
Material:	DVD (Monty Python's Flying Circus Vol. 03, A&E Homevideo), handout / transparency

Sketches

If you and your students relish humorous scenes like that, you may choose another one from Britain's Top 10 chart, which is based on a 2005 poll carried out by Channel 4 (http://news.bbc.co.uk/2/hi/entertainment/4406377.stm).

Britain's Top Ten sketches

No.	*TV show*	*Title*
1	Little Britain	Lou & Andy – At the Pool

2	Monty Python's Flying Circus	Dead Parrot
3	The League of Gentlemen	Tubbs & Edward – Road Men
4	Little Britain	Vicky Pollard – Swimming Pool
5	The Two Ronnies	Four Candles
6	Goodness Gracious Me	Going For An English
7	Victoria Wood – As Seen On TV	Acorn Antiques – Original
8	The Morecambe & Wise Show	Breakfast
9	The Fast Show	Ted & Ralph – Drinking Game
10	Brass Eye	Good Aids/Bad Aids

9.2 Analysing drama

How would you go about analysing a drama?

Approaches to reading a drama

Having selected a drama for your class, you have to decide on which reading approach to take. Similar to dealing with novels (7.3), you can choose between the straight through approach (reading the whole play in advance, followed by classroom discussion of certain topics), segment approach (dividing the play into units, chronological reading and discussing), sandwich approach (reading some parts of the play, leaving out others), select or appetizer approach (choosing only one scene, act, soliloquy, dialogue), single topic approach (reading bits from various plays of the same author, genre, time period, or issue), and patchwork approach (reading excerpts from various sources).

Dramatic competence

Analysing a drama in class is intended to build up the students' *dramatic competence*. This consists of at least three aspects: knowing what to analyse (dimensions of analysis), being familiar with the relevant tools (dramatic terms), and being able to describe these and express one's views (communicative skills).

Drama dimensions

The following table summarises the most important dimensions of drama analysis.

Dimensions of drama analysis	
Genre	Tragedy, comedy, tragicomedy, history play, short play, playlet, sketch etc.
Setting	Time and place, circumstances, mood and atmosphere, props
Plot	Main/sub plots, acts, scenes, stage directions, structure (classic plot: exposition – rising action – climax/turning-point – falling action – resolution), conflicts, comic relief, dramatic irony
Character	Protagonist, (tragic) hero, antagonist, foil, direct/indirect characterization
Theme	Topics, moral/psychological/universal significance, dramatist's view of life, criticism
Language	Prose or verse, style, rhetorical devices, character and language
Evaluation	Overall impression, personal assessment

Drama terms

In order to analyse these dimensions properly, teachers and students alike must be familiar with the most important drama terms, which are described in the following glossary. In order to put some variation, discovery learning and fun into teaching terminology, alternative techniques like crossword puzzles (see Task 3) or error spotting (Task 4) may be employed.

Literary terms: drama	
Act	Main division of a full-length play, consisting of several scenes
Aside	A character's short speech, often in a low voice so that it is not heard by the other characters
Catastrophe	Tragic ending of a play
Climax	Highest point of tension in a play
Comedy	Play intended to amuse, with a happy ending
Comic relief	Short humorous passage that relieves tension in a tragedy
Conflict	Struggle between opposing forces or characters
Dénouement	Last part after climax, in which the conflict is solved (resolution)

Dialogue	Conversation between two or more characters
Dramatic irony	A character does not perceive what his fate holds in store, but the spectator knows better
Exposition	Introduction, setting the action going, suggesting the theme, introducing the main characters, sketching the setting, arousing suspense
Falling action	Action following the climax
Foreshadowing	Verbal and dramatic hints suggesting what is to come later
Monologue	A long speech which is spoken by a single character (he does not need to be alone on the stage)
Motif	A single element (phrase, image, device, incident) frequently repeated to emphasize some aspect of the theme
Playlet	A short play
Props	Articles used on the stage as parts of the scenery
Rising action	Action after the exposition, leading to the climax
Scenery	Overall picture of the stage giving an impression of the place the action is supposed to be happening
Soliloquy	Longer speech, in which sb., alone on the stage, expresses his inner thoughts and feelings
Stage directions	A playwright's written instructions about setting, characters' behaviour etc.
Tragedy	Serious play in which the tragic hero, by his tragic flaw, ends in a final catastrophe
Turning point	Point when an important change takes place (crisis)

Drama phrases

If teachers and students do not have the verbal means to talk about the different dramatic dimensions and terms, communicative interaction in the classroom will fail. Therefore, similar to general classroom phrases, drama phrases must be introduced and learned. The following list may be introduced at some early point of a drama unit and serve as a constant reference point in order to overcome a restricted level of oral and written drama analysis.

Some phrases for drama analysis

- This drama may be classified as a comedy / tragedy because ...
- This play is concerned with the theme of ...
- The playlet is set in ...
- This scene makes use of the following props: ...
- According to the stage instructions the setting is ...
- In the stage directions, the playwright instructs ...
- This play has a closed / open / simple / complex plot.
- This play follows the traditional structure of ...
- The exposition serves to ...
- The complication sets in when ...
- ... constitutes the rising / falling action ...
- The action rises / falls when ...
- The play reaches its climax / crisis / turning point when ...
- This play has a happy / sad / tragic / surprise / open ending.
- The play ends in a catastrophe because ...
- The main conflict is within the character of / between conflicting values / between two characters / the protagonist and society / the hero and fate ...
- The dénouement ends in ...
- The action in this story is predominantly internal / external as ...
- This passage can be seen as comic relief because ...
- Dramatic irony occurs when ... although the audience realizes ...
- In this soliloquy the hero reflects / ponders on ...
- Characterisation here is mainly explicit / implicit ...
- His / Her character is revealed by his / her appearance / words / feelings / behaviour / actions / interactions with / the reactions by / the author's comments ...
- ... is a flat / round / static / dynamic / central / background / intermediate character.
- The protagonist / antagonist / hero / heroine is characterized as ...
- The basic traits of his / her character are ...
- His / Her main features are being friendly (vs. unfriendly), calm (vs. impulsive), reasonable (vs. stubborn), optimistic (vs. pessimistic), content (vs. dissatisfied), altruistic (vs. egotistic)
- ... can be regarded as an anti-hero because ...
- ... acts as a foil to ... in order to highlight the other's positive / negative traits.
- The main / driving motive for ... is ...
- ... stands in clear contrast to ...
- ... is a telling name because ...
- The atmosphere in this scene / passage may be described as bright (vs. dark), serene (vs. mysterious), relaxed (vs. tense), joyful (vs. sad) ...
- The suspense in this scene results from ...

Seeing a performance

A drama should, however, not only be discussed with reference to the intellectual content of the script. Reading ought to be complemented by watching. As a play really comes to life when actors give voice and body to the text, teachers should take their classes to a real performance if possible in order to deepen the understanding of it. A drama must be seen and experienced in the theatre – it is "literature that walks and talks" (Rotter/Bendl 1984: 120).

9.3 Learning by playing

What else, apart from analysing, can you do with plays?

All of us seem to be playing roles in real-life dramas that we are not only starring in but have been scripting, too. We are each the author and leading player in the entertainment called 'My Life'.
Shirley MacLaine

Plays and playing

As dramas are originally written to be acted out, Shakespeare and many other playwrights would probably turn in their graves if they could see the tortured way in which students are frequently asked to dissect their texts without even so much as a few minutes action during the lesson. Nünning's epigrammatic title *From 'Teaching Drama' to 'Teaching Plays'* (1998) makes us aware of the double meaning of *play*, i.e. both a piece of theatre and doing things you enjoy. Our learners are used to playing from early childhood, and using plays in class does not only improve their reading and speaking skills, but encourages creativity, makes them experiment with oral, written and body language, brings them out of themselves, and can involve the whole class. As the term *play* covers a wide area of techniques which classrooms often lack, including vocal action, physical movement, and mental concentration, the possibilities for learning by playing are countless.

Theatre and playing

This does not only mean the big theatre performance at the end of the school year, but begins with reading a short coursebook dialogue with different roles and acting it out in front of the class. The following table compares drama in the theatre with playing in the classroom.

Theatre	Playing
Drama	Plays, textbook dialogue ... school performance
Stage	Classroom, school premises
Scenery	Furniture of classroom, chairs, tables, simple props
Actors	Students, teacher
Director	Teacher, student
Drama script	Idea, material, story, scenario, writing one's own script
Rehearse	Read, experiment with, practise, show, explore, work on

Perform	Improvise, show, act out, dramatize
Audience	School-mates, peers, parents, teachers
Critique	Discuss, evaluate
PRODUCT	PROCESS

Short and longer activities

This table demonstrates the great scope and potential of plays and playing. Students may use a given script (e.g. a short narrative based on brief scenes of 2 lines, a humorous sketch, a play broken up with songs, a two-scene playlet dealing with a familiar story), or write and do their own play (e.g. start from a photo or music video, invent a one-act play based on popular film characters, transform a short story into a radio play). A very successful form is the so-called *Reader's Theatre*: exciting short plays, freely available, suitable from primary up to adult learners, from four characters to whole-class participation, working from a script which is first read at the front of the class (www.teachingheart.net/readerstheater.htm). Further activities can be found in numerous books and journal articles (Maley/Duff 1982, Ladousse 1987, Wessels 1987, Scheller 1981, Meyer 1997, Wilkening 1998, Bludau 2000).

A big performance

There are also a few sound reasons for spending a considerable amount of time on preparing a bigger performance. Students learn whole chunks of language in a clear context, plays are memorable and so beyond learning their own parts they are often able to say the others' parts, too, students can demonstrate skills usually neglected in the language classroom, the best performers are not always the strongest students, the performance provides satisfaction for students and parents alike to see how much language they can produce, and the whole process often turns out to be a great bonding experience for a class. The suggestions in the following flow chart may help teachers to prepare for the big night (Scheller 1981, Maley/Duff 1982, Frost 2007).

Tips for a class play	
Stages	*Do's*
Finding an idea	• Think of a current topic. • Look back at the coursebook topics. • Adapt a familiar story. • Work from a given script.
▼	
Fixing the date	• Plan a performance for parents, school, or class exchange. • Set a deadline as motivation to work.
▼	
Writing the play	• Put up pictures of people and have the students invent profiles. • Discuss the relationships between the characters and the basic plot. • Make the students write the basic outline of the plot. • Correct and edit the drafts and use this stage for language work.
▼	
Choosing roles	• Start by asking for volunteers. • Give them the chance to audition for different roles. • Involve the whole class. • Offer non-speaking roles to shy students. • Give technical roles to those interested (lighting, sound, props, scenery, prompting)
▼	
Remembering the lines	• Get them to read through aloud. • Test their comprehension by making gaps or putting in mistakes (gap-filling, error-spotting). • Break the script into chunks of learning. • Have the learners mark their scripts (highlighting stressed words, intonation etc.). • Record/videotape a rehearsal to look at together. • Do a performance in front of some other people.
▼	
Performing the play	• Create a good atmosphere and nice surroundings. • Video it and take photographs.

The whole process from the first idea to the big night may be quite time-consuming and nerve-racking, but experience shows that it is very rewarding.

Tasks

1. Choose one title from the British Top Ten sketches and do the following tasks:
   a) Research some background information on your sketch.
   b) Find a way to watch it.
   c) Decide whether you are going to use it in your classes.
2. Crossword puzzle: Find the corresponding drama terms for the following definitions:
   Across:
   1 main division of a drama
   3 short humorous passage within a tragedy (2 words)
   4 when students create a scene and freeze the action (2 words)
   5 a type of short performance
   6 time and place of a play
   9 short play
   10 another word for dénouement
   Down:
   2 another word for crisis (2 words)
   7 highest point of tension in a play
   8 articles on the stage

3. British drama: error spotting
   The following summary of the historical development of British drama contains one mistake. Identify it and correct it.

The development of British drama

The decisive impulse for the beginnings of English drama came from within the church. The Mystery plays of the late Middle Ages centred around the Crucifixion and Resurrection, the Miracle plays dramatized episodes from the lives of saints. The Bible as the basis of drama was given up in the Morality plays, which presented the struggle between good and evil in man's soul, and showed vices and virtues as allegorical figures on the stage, e.g. Everyman (c. 1490).

The great age of English drama came with the movement of the Renaissance. The University Wits, a group of young dramatists associated with the universities of Oxford and Cambridge (Thomas Kyd, Christopher Marlowe), laid the foundations for the later comedy of romance and the conception of tragedy. Troupes of strolling players formed professional acting companies, and permanent public theatres began to be stablished from 1576 onwards. It was against this background that William Shakespeare started writing plays and becoming the greatest dramatist in world literature. It is somehow unfortunate that his towering shadow has obscured the rich contributions of his contemporaries and successors – Ben Jonson's comedies of humours, Fletcher's and Beaumont's comedies of London life, Webster's sinister tragedies. When the theatres were closed in 1642, the richest era of English drama was brought to an end.

The drama of the Restoration period, of the 18th century and much of the 19th century put the focus on lighthearted and superficial entertainment. The Restoration comedy of manners shows elegant ladies and gentlemen of fashion and rank in their conversations and amorous intrigues. 18th century drama stresses sentimentality and tearfulness. The renewal of drama in the 19th century was mainly brought about by Oscar Wilde, who revived the spirit of the comedy of manners (e.g. The Importance of Being Earnest), satirized conventional morality and excelled in verbal wit. Another Irishman, George Bernard Shaw, presented a drama of ideas and philosophical comedies. Verse drama experienced a remarkabale renaissance in the 1930s and 40s. T.S. Eliot gave a big stimulus to poetic drama (Murder in the Cathedral), Christopher Fry delighted his audience with his verbal dexterity (The Lady's not for Burn-

ing). The beginning of a new chapter in the history of English drama was marked when John Osborne's Look Back in Anger premiered in 1956. The figure of Jimmy Porter belongs to the Angry Young Men and is the first anti-Establishment hero in modern English drama, who is disillusioned and uses uninhibited language. The New Wave or kitchen-sink drama inspired scores of new dramatists who shared a keen sense of new dramatic possibilities: Wesker, Bond, Arden, Stoppard, Pinter. The latter, who was strongly influenced by the Theatre of the Absolute (Beckett: Waiting for Godot, 1954), received the Nobel Prize for Literature in 2005 – maybe 35 years too late.

adapted from: Rotter/Bendl 1984: 162 – 224

4. Choose one of the resource books or articles mentioned in 9.3 and find out what activities for plays and playing it describes: Maley/Duff 1982, Ladousse 1987, Wessels 1987, Scheller 1981, Meyer 1997, Wilkening 1998, Bludau 2000.

10 Shakespeare

10.1 Shakespeare for all

What didn't you like about your Shakespeare lessons at school?

Arguments for Shakespeare

There are many reasons why William Shakespeare should be taught in English language classrooms (Gibson 1998). In terms of his literary and cultural status, the Man of the Millennium is still No 1 in the English speaking world. So the answer to the question as to why we should teach the Bard, must be "Who else?" This outstanding position has to do with the universality of the themes he treats and the characters he depicts. "Shakespeare is for all ages," as his contemporary Ben Jonson once stated. Studying Shakespeare helps the learner to develop both cognitive and affective skills. Apart from knowledge, personal attributes like empathy, imagination or judgement are strengthened as Shakespeare develops "the understanding heart". Moreover for the foreign language learners the poet and playwright from Avon serves as a model and resource which fosters their linguistic development. Finally the Bard fascinates us through his otherness, i.e. he is extraordinary in the way he blends the familiar and the strange, and juxtaposes different beliefs, values and ways of living.

Barriers: author and methodology

Yet teaching Shakespeare in classrooms has always been a problem which derives both from the author and the methodology used. The Stratford man wrote his plays and sonnets more than 400 years ago in early modern English, which in several ways is different to the modern English language. So his Elizabethan dramas are characterized by a rather elaborated style full of complex rhetorical devices. Despite Jonson's claim the historical distance has made some of his plots and topics hard to understand. The widespread bardolatry has also contributed to an attitude of awe and respect which may hinder an open and relaxed study of his works. Beyond author-related problems the methodoloy often employed in Shakespeare classes has met with criticism. An author-centred approach, whose main goal is to find out the writer's intention by analysing all the lines in detail and finally providing a single true interpretation, has dominated many lessons. The study of a Shakespeare drama often lasted too many weeks and was confined to the printed text, neglecting other related media. Given all these conditions it is no wonder that many students experienced a loss of motivation.

New theoretical approaches

In the last few decades new theoretical approaches and methods of textual and cultural interpretation have emerged, however, which challenge traditional procedures. *Post-structuralism* and *Deconstructivism* (Jacques Derrida, Michel Foucault, Julia Kristeva) view culture as integral to every textual work, claim that the meaning of any work is itself a cultural phenomenon, and state that the meaning the author intended is secondary to the meaning that the reader perceives. Instead of the idea of a literary text having one purpose, one meaning or one singular existence, a variety of perspectives is utilized to create a multifaceted interpretation of a text. In this process of *destabilizing* or *decentering* the author, the reader replaces the author as the primary subject of inquiry.

Another approach to literary criticism is *New Historicism*, which developed in the 1980s (Stephen Greenblatt) and fought against the New Criticism of formal analysis of literature. It holds that a literary work should not be regarded as an isolated creation of genius but rather a product of the time, place and circumstances of its composition. According to *Cultural materialism* the infrastructure of a society (material relations) determines the structure (social relations), which determines the superstructure (ideological relations including literature). The Russian literary critic Michail Bachtin paves the way for *intertextuality* by stressing the fact that every spoken or written word is a dialogue with other words and texts and thus full of different meanings. "Jedes Wort (jedes Zeichen) eines Textes führt über seine Grenzen hinaus. Jedes Verstehen ist das In-Beziehung-Setzen des jeweiligen Textes mit anderen Texten ... Der Text lebt nur, indem er sich mit einem anderen Text berührt" (Bachtin 1979: 352). *Performance and Theatre Studies* as well as *Film Studies* finally go beyond the written Shakespeare text and explore the dramatic and cinematic aspects of his works.

Methodological consequences

All these new approaches to literary criticism have far-reaching methodological implications for the classroom (Antor 1997, Klose 2000, Bergmann/Kroth 2002, Petersohn/Volkmann 2005). Long cherished analytical categories like subject, intention, meaning, message, truth, text, or authenticity have become dubious. We have to say farewell to the notion that a text releases "a single 'theological' meaning (the 'message' of the Author-God)", as Barthes proposes in his *Death of the Author* (1967). Teachers have to accept the open, dynamic, and polysemous nature of literary texts and be open to a variety of interpretations. It is up to the readers, i.e. the students, to ascribe meanings to the texts and justify their personal interpretations. As a consequence the learners in the classroom have to be activated via process-oriented, student-centred and action-oriented techniques to find their own way towards Shakespeare. In this process the concepts of intertextuality and intermediality should play a vital role, original Shakespeare texts can be read in connection with related modern texts and various media.

Shakespeare for all

Such an approach makes Shakespeare suitable for all media, texts, methods ... and ages, i.e. not only historical periods, but all age groups among our learners. Using Shakespeare with younger learners, of course, requires different texts and methods, e.g. simplified readers, short and simple plot summaries, games, interesting information about his life, story telling, graphic summaries, matching English and German titles of his plays, crossword puzzles, making a fictitious dialogue with him and other creative activities (Schroeder-Thürauf 2006, Gehring 1997). "Those that do teach young babes do it with gentle means and easy tasks" (Othello, IV,ii).

A *Shakespeare for all* approach combines various forms of *closed teaching* and *open learning*, aiming at the double goal of understanding and enjoying Shakespeare (cf. illustration).

Shakespeare for all

Closed Teaching		*Open Learning*
– teacher-fronted – quarto/folio text – traditional media – intensive reading – close analysis – deskbound approach – advanced level		– student-centred – intertextuality – intermediality – skimming & scanning – creation & extension – workshop approach – all ages

▼

understanding & enjoying
Shakespeare

Shakespeare for all media

Due to his popularity and relevance the works of Shakespeare have been made use of in various media. For example, the following survey lists 30 media formats for *Hamlet*, showing us that working with Shakespeare does not have to be reduced to reading the text only.

Shakespeare for all media

Medium	*Example (Hamlet)*
Printed text	Quarto, folio, hybrid
Audio book	Arkangel Shakespeare: *Hamlet*
Stage play	Visiting a performance
Simplified reader	The Young Reader's Shakespeare: *Hamlet*
Picture book	Barron's Picture This! Shakespeare Series: *Hamlet*
Comics reference	*Hagar*
Animated cartoon	*The Lion King* (1994, Simba as Hamlet, Scar as Claudius)
Musical	*Hair* (1967, *What a Piece of Work is Man*)
Classical music	Franz Liszt, *Hamlet* (1858), symphonic poem
Opera	Domenico Scarlatti, *Ambleto* (1715)
Painting	Joseph Stella: *Ophelia* (1926)
Pop music	Dream Theater: *Pull Me Under*
Music video	Nick Cave & Kylie Minogue: *Where the Wild Roses Grow*
Television	BBC Television Shakespeare: *Hamlet*
Cinema	Laurence Olivier, *Hamlet* (1948)
Posters	Schöningh: *The New Summit* (various film posters)
Film reference	*Star Trek VI: The Undiscovered Country* (1991)
Sketch	*Monty Python's Flying Circus*, episode 43
Sitcom	*The Simpsons*, episode 14
Stage summary	Tom Stoppard: *The Fifteen Minute Hamlet*
Stage reference	Tom Stoppard: *Rosencrantz & Guildenstern Are Dead*
Prose fiction	James Joyce: *Ulysses*, episode 9

Web spoof	www.angelfire.com/oh/Pretzel/
Email exchange	Class exchange project with a British school
Hypertext project	Creating a class website
CD ROM	The Arden Shakespeare: *Hamlet. CD-ROM*
Forum/newsgroup	http://shakespeareforums.com/forumdisplay.php?f=33
Chatbot	ALICE (http://www.alicebot.org/)
WebQuest	http://ods.schule.de/englisch/webquest/hamlet/index.htm
Computer game	Ensemble Studios, *Age of Empires III* (reference to III, 1)

10.2 Shakespeare's time

What do you know about the chain of being, the proscenium stage, and the pronouns in early modern English?

Researching his background

Shakespeare's works can only be understood and truly enjoyed if one knows a little about the socio-cultural and political background of his era. Therefore it is necessary to make students acquainted with his life, other works, the Elizabethan Age, the theatre of his times, the language spoken then, and the dominant views of the world. This information can be provided by the teacher bit by bit when needed, by the students in the form of individual lectures, or via audiovisual formats. Another idea is to have the learners research, prepare and present the Shakespearean context in six groups, each dealing with a different aspect and guided by research tasks. The students may use private books, public libraries or the Internet, the product of their work could be a *Focus on Facts* two-page print-out, a wall display or a powerpoint presentation (cf. teaching unit, Thaler 2007c).

Teaching Unit	
Topic:	Shakespeare's Time
Aims:	researching, presenting, integrated skills
Level:	from grade 11
Time:	four 45-minute lessons
Procedure:	– 1st lesson: introduction, forming groups, research – 2nd lesson: preparing the presentation – 3rd and 4th lessons: presentation of six groups
Materials:	research tasks, Internet links, presentation tools
Research tasks:	*Group 1: His life* • What are the most important dates in his life? Why? • Where did he live? How? • Are there any unsolved secrets? Group 2: His works • What genres of books did he cover? • What are the most important works? • Are there any rumours about the authorship? Group 3: His age • Why is this period called The Elizabethan Age? • What were the basic structures of politics and society? • What role did the monarch play in Shakespeare's life? Group 4: His theatre • What did a theatre look like in that age? • In what ways was it different to today's stage? • What role did a playwright have in that era? Group 5: His world view • What is the chain of being? • What did the wheel of fortune mean for the common man? • What is the idea of humours about? • What was the people's attitude towards supernatural appearances? *Group 6: His language* Describe the main features of Early Modern English on the levels of • phonology • lexis and imagery • syntax
Internet links:	www.Shakespeare.com www.Shakespeare-online.com www.luminarium.org/renlit/eliza.htm

10.3 Shakespeare's sonnets

Is it really vital to teach 16th century sonnets to 21st century teenagers?

Arguments for sonnets

According to Jarfe (2005), there are at least three reasons for integrating Shakespeare sonnets into TEFL. If no original Shakespeare play can be read in class, sonnets serve as a substitute introducing learners to the Bard's exceptional language. If the genre of sonnets is the topic in class, a Shakespeare sonnet should be among the examples illustrating this genre, as the Bard has led this form to its completion. Lastly, some of his sonnets are among the most popular, cited and discussed poems of the English language, having reached a sort of cult status (e.g. No. 18 and 116).

Selecting suitable sonnets

Their use being justified, the question arises as to which sonnets the teacher should choose. Apart from popularity, there are some other criteria of selection. They should not be too demanding in terms of their lingusitic, thematic and intertextual complexity (so beware of No. 20 or No. 107). Moreover the teacher should opt for humorous and satirical examples (e.g. No. 130) rather than serious and solemn ones. As the form of the poem is also a matter of analytical interest, the sonnet should clearly illustrate the typical features of the Shakespearean/Elizabethan type (*turn* or *volta* after the third quatrain, epigrammatic character of the couplet) or be a synthesis of the Italian/Petrarchan and the English/Elizabethan types (No. 18). Finally the great, universal themes of mankind such as love, transitoriness and death (No. 18, No. 65, No. 116, No. 130, No. 147) are more appealing to students than motifs peculiar to the Elizabethan Age.

Methods and tasks

As far as the methodological procedure in class is concerned, a traditional analysis of form, content and message has not lost its place in an English language classroom. Several print and online sources help the teacher by giving him/her the full texts inluding annotations and commentaries (e.g. www.shakespeare-online.com/sonnets). The English original can be compared to (various) German translations (Schuenke 1999, Taubenböck 2006). A contrastive analysis of two Shakespeare sonnets which treat the same topic with different tone and intention can also be rewarding (e.g. the love topic in the cult sonnets No. 18 and No. 130).

William Shakespeare: **Sonnet 18**

Shall I compare thee to a summer's day?
Thou art more lovely and more temperate:
Rough winds do shake the darling buds of May,
And summer's lease hath all too short a date:
Sometime too hot the eye of heaven shines,
And oft' is his gold complexion dimm'd;
And every fair from fair sometime declines,
By chance or nature's changing course untrimm'd:
But thy eternal summer shall not fade
Nor lose possession of that fair thou owest;
Nor shall death brag thou wanderest in his shade,
When in eternal lines to time thou growest:
So long as men can breathe, or eyes can see,
So long lives this, and this gives life to thee.

William Shakespeare: **Sonnet 130**

My mistress' eyes are nothing like the sun;
Coral is far more red than her lips' red;
If snow be white, why then her breasts are dun;
If hairs be wires, black wires grow on her head.
I have seen roses damask'd, red and white,
But no such roses see I in her cheeks;
And in some perfumes is there more delight
Than in the breath that from my mistress reeks.
I love to hear her speak, yet well I know
That music hath a far more pleasing sound;
I grant I never saw a goddess go;
My mistress, when she walks, treads on the ground:
And yet, by heaven, I think my love as rare
As any she belied with false compare.

Modern approaches

Alternative and creative techniques should complement the conventional approaches. There are various ideas the teacher can try out:

- Comparison of original and modern English version (www.shakespeare-online.com/sonnets)
- Comparing various tongue-in-cheek translations such as radically modernist or dialect versions (Taubenböck 2006: 193ff.)
- Comparison with a modern poem dealing with the same topic (e.g. No. 18 and Adrian Henry's *Love Is*)
- Comparison with a pop song (e.g. No. 130 and Tom Lehrer's *When You're Old and Grey*)

- Comparing original, modern translation, audio translation and song (e.g. Wolf Biermann's translations and songs, 2005)
- Students writing their own (modern English) sonnet
- Staging a sonnet slam

Adrian Henri: **Love Is ...**	
Love is feeling cold in the back of vans Love is a fanclub with only two fans Love is walking holding paintstained hands Love is. Love is fish and chips on winter nights Love is blankets full of strange delights Love is when you don't put out the light Love is Love is the presents in Christmas shops Love is when you're feeling Top of the Pops Love is what happens when the music stops Love is	Love is white panties lying all forlorn Love is pink nightdresses still slightly warm Love is when you have to leave at dawn Love is Love is you and love is me Love is prison and love is free Love's what's there when you are away from me Love is...

Tom Lehrer: **When you're old and grey**	
Since I still appreciate you, Let's find love while we may. Because I know I'll hate you When you are old and grey. So say you love me here and now, I'll make the most of that. Say you love and trust me, For I know you'll disgust me When you're old and getting fat. An awful debility, A lessened utility, A loss of mobility Is a strong possibility. In all probability I'll lose my virility And you your fertility And desirability.	And this liability Of total sterility Will lead to hostility And a sense of futility. So let's act with agility While we still have facility, For we'll soon reach senility And lose the ability. Your teeth will start to go, dear, Your waist will start to spread. In twenty years or so, dear, I'll wish that you were dead. I'll never love you then at all The way I do today. So please remember, When I leave in December, I told you so in May.

10.4 Shakespeare's plays

Which of Shakespeare's dramas did you read at school?

His most popular plays

Which are the most popular Shakespeare plays? Looking at the Top Ten list of all dramas read in German classrooms (see 9.1), one finds *Macbeth* at No. 1 leading with a wide margin; more than half of the German students interviewed had studied the tragedy of the ambitious Scottish nobleman. Among the other Shakespeare plays, *Romeo and Juliet*, *Julius Caesar*, *Hamlet* and *The Merchant of Venice* take the next places, read by between 5 and 9 % each. The popularity of *Macbeth* may be due to the relative brevity of the play, its rather straight plot, the themes of violence and ambition, and the fact that teachers teach what they have been taught – plus the publishers' great amount of *Macbeth* resources. Whether the Shakespeare boom in the 1990s with its spectacular film adaptions of comedies and slightly less popular plays leads to a shift in the selection of dramas for school use remains to be seen.

Ways of reading his plays

As to the mode of presentation in class, teachers have the same choice of basic approaches as with plays in general (cf. 9). They may go for a straight through, segment, sandwich, clip – or appetizer approach. The latter selects a few scenes from various plays, illustrating different topics and genres, combined with some information on the author and his times (Thaler 2007c).

Literary and dramatic approaches

No matter which mode they choose, teachers can opt for literary or dramatic approaches to teaching Shakespeare. The first is the traditional or textual way of reading Shakespeare and implies a deskbound student who is rather passive while reading. Rex Gibson and his influential *Shakespeare and Schools Project* at Cambridge have replaced the literary approach in many British schools by their dramatic approach, wanting the plays to be taught as plays, since Shakespeare wrote them to be acted (Gibson 1998, Stredder 2006). They believe that children understand, experience and appreciate the Bard's plays more profoundly if they are involved in their dramatic presentation. This may mean devising a rough-and-ready class performance which observes the spirit of Elizabethan theatre, or role-playing a few selected scenes, or creating modern adaptations and diversions from the original text. Jeffcoate rejects the polarisation of literary and dramatic approaches and argues instead for a combined literary-dramatic approach "for the simple reason that Shakespeare plays are both literary and dramatic texts (and have been at least since the publication of the First Folio in 1623) and hence demand and repay both dramatic enactment and literary study" (2002:11).

Teaching materials

School publishing companies help the teacher who has decided on one of these approaches by offering a variety of readers – from a 44-page simplified version of *The Tempest* for beginners (Cornelsen Verlag) to fully annotated, task-accompanied and drama-oriented *Oxford* and *Cambridge School Shakespeares* or Schöningh's *Discover Shakespeare* doubles (textbook including activities plus teacher's book). On the Internet numerous websites provide (commented) link collections (gateways such as www.aerslynx.org/theatre/shakes.htm), the whole original texts (e.g. the fast and stable access of the MIT: www-tech.mit.edu/Shakespeare/works.html) and tested teaching aids (in particular the numerous student-centred teaching ideas of the Folger Library: www.folger.edu/education/getarchive.cfm).

Hamlet and intermediality

In the following the Bard's most often staged play *Hamlet* (Hazlitt: *Hamlet, that's us*), will be used to illustrate several alternative ways of using a Shakespeare play in combination with various media – trying to take the concepts of intertextuality and intermediality seriously.

Simplified readers

Simplified readers (stage readers, adapted readers) such as the *Shakespeare can be fun* series (Firefly) allow *Hamlet* to be read by children. Such nicely illustrated, lexically and structurally simplified versions of great classics prove that *you're never too young for Shakespeare*. They are suitable for stand alone use with lower grades or as a reading and comprehension aid for higher grades, used side by side with the original version. An inter-genre comparison could compare the original and the simplified version, an intra-genre comparison needs two different simplified readers of *Hamlet*.

Paintings

Hamlet's Ophelia has become the favourite character for painters of all ages. Numerous paintings portray her madness and death, for example Dante Gabriel Rossetti, John William Waterhouse, Joseph Stella and, of course, John Everett Millais. After students have read the account of Ophelia's death, they may be asked to imagine the circumstances of her death, before they go on to study Millais' *Ophelia* (1852, Tate Gallery, reproductions on many websites) in three steps – description, analysis, and evaluation based on the reading of the text. This 19th century painting may afterwards be compared with a 20th century one such as the one by Stella.

Film adaptations

Moving from still to moving pictures, a way of motivating a class is to compare the text and the corresponding film version. As *Hamlet* has often been adapted on screen, choosing one scene (e.g. Hamlet's famous hesitation in III.iii or the mousetrap scene in III.ii) and comparing different movie adaptations yields revealing insights into different interpretations and the protagonist's ambiguous character (Kamp 2006). Four of the most famous films may be chosen, starting with the great Sir Laurence Olivier in the classical black-and-white version of 1948. Action star Mel Gibson has the title role in Franco Zeffirelli's adaptation of 1990. Kenneth Branagh's 1996 film is notable for being the first unabridged screen version of the play (slightly over four hours); it is set with Victorian era costuming and furnishings, has a strong visual appeal, resorts to silent flashbacks and dream sequences for the many monologues, and shows a large number of celebrity cameos. The setting of Michael Almereyda's *Hamlet* (2000) is contemporary Manhattan, with Ethan Hawke playing the hero as a film student with a laptop amidst a high-tech world of video cameras and surveillance bugs.

Sitcoms

Not only full-length feature films, but also shorter sitcoms have taken up the *Hamlet* story. The famous *Simpsons*, with Homer as King Hamlet and Bart as the young prince, re-enact the drama in six minutes as an animated cartoon (*Tales from the Public Domain*, episode 14, season 13, 2002). Having read the whole *Hamlet*, students may enjoy this animated synopsis, identify deviations from the original, and finally write a Hamlet plot for another sitcom of their choice.

The Simpsons: Hamlet *(beginning)*

Homer: Our next story is "Hamlet" by William Shakespeare.
Bart: Dad, this writer can't compare with our modern superwriters. Stephen Bosco could kick Shakespeare's ass!
Lisa: No, this story is more interesting than you think. It starts with Hamlet's father getting murdered.
Bart: Cool. Does he get to marry his mom?
Homer: I don't know, but that would be hot. …

Sketches

The legendary British comedy group Monty Python have turned Hamlet's procrastination into a hilarious sketch (*Monty Python's Flying Circus*, episode 43, 1974). The Pythonesque Hamlet (Terry Jones) lies on the couch of a modern psychiatrist's office complaining: "It's just that everywhere I go it's the same old thing. All anyone wants me to say is 'To be or not to be!'". Several bogus psychiatrists try to cure Hamlet's depression with the help of pseudo-Freudian psycho-analysis. This sketch can be viewed, analysed with respect to British humour, and finally lead to a role play, in which students take the roles of the psychiatrist and Hamlet in a double circle (*Kugellager*).

Pop songs

The Danish prince has also found his way into modern pop music. The progressive rock track *Pull Me Under* by Dream Theater delineates in its lyrics Hamlet's view of life and his conflict between revenge and sanity. The lack of an ending – the song stops mid-note after eight minutes – is meant to emphasize the theme of the song by demonstrating how quickly life can end. To practise the students' listening comprehension, a *mondegreen* version of the song can be presented: Ten words of the lyrics are replaced by mishearings or *Freudsche Verhörer*, e.g. "his Fred" for "afraid", and students have to detect and correct the mistakes while listening. In a post-listening phase they may be asked to describe Hamlet's state of mind using the ten words from the lyrics.

Dream Theater: **Pull Me Under**

Lost in the sky
Clouds roll by and I roll with them
Arrows fly
Seas increase and then fall again

This world is spinning around me
This world is spinning without me
Every day sends future to past
Every breath leaves one less to my last

Watch the sparrow falling
Gives new meaning to it all
If not today nor yet tomorrow
then some other day

I'll take seven lives for one
And then my only father's son

Pull me under Pull me under
Pull me under I'm not afraid
All that I feel is honor and spite
All I can do is to set it right

Dust fills my eyes
Clouds roll by and I roll with them
Centuries cry
Orders fly and I fall again

This world is spinning inside me
The whole world is spinning inside of me
Every day sends future to past
Every step brings me closer to my last

Pull me under Pull me under
Pull me under I'm not afraid

As sure as I ever did love him I am not afraid This world is spinning ...	Living my life too much in the sun Only until your will is done 'Oh that this too too solid flesh would melt.'

Music videos

Music videos add a visual dimension to the text and music. The famous clip *Where the Wild Roses Grow* by Nick Cave & Kylie Minogue, a murder ballad and alternative rock song, displays several references to Hamlet, Ophelia and Ophelia paintings in terms of setting, characters, plot and symbolism – although not openly admitted by its makers. After students have watched this music video, they can analyse parallels and differences between Ophelia's death and the murder scene in the video, before the teacher proceeds to study cinematic techniques such as camera angles, camera movements and shots – possibly with the help of a five-column grid (scene number, actors, camera, field size, action).

Spoofs

Hamlet's *to-be-or-not-to-be* soliloquy (III.i) is one of the most popular icons of Western civilization. It is no wonder that it has also inspired modern writers to parody these lines. A wonderful collection of spoofs created by grade 12 students can be found at www.angelfire.com/oh/Pretzel/. After students have studied the original soliloquy and read a few parodies, they may be able to write their own spoofs, the best of which are then published on the school homepage or at www.angelfire.

The Slacker's Soliloquy

To slack, or not to slack, that is the question;
Whether 'tis nobler in the mind to suffer
The zeros and low marks of outrageous assignments,
Or to take pens against a sea of compositions,
And by opposing, finish them. To work; to accomplish,
No more, and by accomplishment to say we end
The workload, and the thousand essays
That students are heirs to; 'tis a dream
Devoutly to be wish'd. To work, to accomplish;
To accomplish; perchance to succeed; ay, there's the rub;
For in that accomplishment of work what mark may come,

When we have submitted this completed piece,
Must give us pause; there's the respect
That makes calamity of so long a school career.
Enoch Tung

Tasks

1. The 30 media formats, based on *Hamlet*, demonstrate that Shakespeare is for all media. Choose three of them and do some research to find out how they can be used in class.
2. The research into Shakespeare's background is divided into six groups. Choose one group and do the tasks given.
3. Compare sonnet 18 and sonnet 130 answering the following questions:
   a) Who might the addressees of the two poems be?
   b) What formal aspects do the two sonnets have in common?
   c) How do they differ as to content and intention?
4. Write a modern version of the III, 1 soliloquy. Possible titles are *the student's soliloquy, the teacher's soliloquy, the eater's soliloquy, the boozer's soliloquy, the traveller's soliloquy*.

About Literature

11 Modern media

11.1 Forms and functions

How can media contribute to literary communicative competence?

Personal and non-personal media

Media have always played an important part in the English language classroom. As far as different forms are concerned, a first distinction may be made between personal media, i.e. the teacher and the learners, and instructional (non-personal) media, e.g. literary readers, handouts with literary terms, or theatre performances.

Modes of perception

An even more common way of differentiating media is to arrange them according to the senses they relate to. We have got visual media, such as the blackboard / whiteboard (to summarize the results of classroom discussions), worksheets (with literary terms or analysis tasks), transparencies for the overhead projector (with graphic representations of plot or character constellations), slides, photos and pictures (of authors, stages, historical background). Then there are auditory media, e.g. audio-cassettes, CDs, audio-books (with the original texts spoken by professional actors). The audio-visual media comprise films, videos and DVDs (of literary adaptations). In particular the development of *digital versatile discs*, with the options of subtitles, different languages, direct scene access, and bonus tracks, has widened the scope for integrating media, language, culture and literature (Thaler 2001). A fourth form of media has evolved with the advent of computers and Internet. Interactive formats which can enrich the literature classroom are, among others, hypertexts, email and forums.

Variety of functions

All these media can fulfil various functions in literature lessons. They are employed

- to serve as a tool for language instruction
- to create a more authentic learning environment
- to bring in native speakers in voice and image
- to improve listening skills, listening-viewing skills and non-verbal communication skills
- to foster intercultural learning
- to support a learner-centred learning process
- to contribute to information literacy / media literacy / electronic literacy

Thus, with the help of different media, literature may help to support what the New London Group has termed *multiliteracies* (Cope/Kalantzis 2000: 3ff.). According to this international team of interdisciplinary researchers, there is a *multiplicity of communications channels and media*, which forces students to learn how to deal with different forms of communication and not be content with the written-linguistic code only.

Multi-literacies

11.2 Literature & Music

Music and literature – a dichotomy?

Music and song have proved to be of enormous motivational potential in English language classrooms (cf. the *A-Dekalog* in Thaler 1999:134ff.). Songs are attractive, authentic, up-to-date teaching material (*Attraktivität, Authentizität, Aktualität*), which provide a change from everyday routine (*Abwechslung*), are omnipresent (*Allgegenwärtigkeit*), reflect young people's concerns (*Adressatenorientierung*), are part of teenagers' daily lives (*Anwendbarkeit*), work as *teddy-bear-in-the-ear* or as *ersatz-lover-mother* (*Affektivität*), are suitable for discursive negotiations of meaning due to their semantic ambiguity (*Auslegbarkeit*), and can foster student-centred learning (*Aktivität*).

A-Dekalog

Moreover music meets literature in several ways. Faulstich (1978) regards pop lyrics as *modern mass poetry*, Lorch (1988) interprets the music video *Money for Nothing* by Dire Straits as a *neo-metaphysical poem*, some song texts are worthy of literary analysis, and Duxbury (1988) has found a lot of literary allusions and references in rock music (table: Thaler 1999: 161).

Music meets literature

Allusions in pop music to literature

Type of reference	*Pop music*	*Literature*
1. Singers and bands a) Author	– Bob Dylan – Keats – H.P. Lovecraft – Shakespeare's Sisters – Shelleyan Orphan	– Dylan Thomas – J. Keats – H.P.Lovecraft – W. Shakespeare – P.B. Shelley

b) Title of novel	– Bram Stoker – Soft Machine – Supertramp	– B. Stoker – Burroughs: *The Soft Machine* – Davies: *The Autobiography of a Super-Tramp*
c) Character in novel	– Uriah Heep – Artful Dodger – Eloy	– Dickens: *David Copperfield* – Dickens: *Oliver Twist* – Wells: *The Time Machine*
d) Short story	Icicle Works	Pohl: *The Day the Icicle Works Closed*
e) Drama	Twelfth Night	Shakespeare: *Twelfth Night*
f) Poem	Ravyns	E. A. Poe: *The Raven*
2. Titles of songs and albums	– Bush: Wuthering Heights – Dire Straits: Romeo & Juliet – T. Dolby: Byronic Love – FGTH: Rage Hard – FGTH: Welcome to the Pleasuredome – Sting: Nothing Like the Sun	– Bronte: *Wuthering Heights* – Shakespeare: *Romeo and Juliet* – Lord Byron – Thomas: *Do Not Go Gentle Into That Good Night* – Coleridge: *Kubla Khan* – Shakespeare: *Sonnet 130*
3. Song lyrics	– Stewart: Every Picture Tells a Story – Stevens: Morning Has Broken	– references to Dickens, Shelley, Keats – Farjeon: *A Morning Song*
4. Concept albums	– Eurythmics: 1984 – Alan Parsons Project: Tales of Mystery and Imagination	– Orwell: *1984* – Poe: various stories and poems
5. Visual references (music videos)	– Men at Work: Dr Heckyll and Mr Jive – T. Petty: Don't Come Around Here No More – Ravyns: Rhythm of the Heart	– Stevenson: *Dr Jekyll and Mr Hyde* – Carroll: *Alice in Wonderland* – E.A. Poe's historic house

3 approaches to teaching music

All those inter-textual references may be exploited in the classroom (Thaler 2009a). Depending on the teacher's objectives, he or she may give a quick talk on the parallels, have students prepare short presentations on the authors or sources cited, analyse the source (in excerpts) or compare song / music video with the literary text. When teachers want to work with songs and music videos in more detail, they can employ one of the following three general approaches to music. The *global-to-detailed approach* calls for listening to a song twice and proceeds from a global comprehension to a detailed understanding of the song. The *pwp approach* structures the lesson into a pre-listening (viewing), while-listening (viewing) and a post-listening (viewing) stage. The *code-referenced approach* is based on the various codes a song or video is composed of and invites teachers to choose those codes they want to focus on.

Code-referenced approach: Dire Straits song

To illustrate the code-referenced approach, let us take the song and corresponding music video *Romeo & Juliet*, which is taken from the Dire Straits' third album *Making Movies* (1980), still holding top positions in polls today. The song takes up the *Romeo and Juliet* motif and transforms it into everyday British life. Working with the written text here can mean identifying the poetic form (ballad, pseudo-romantic ode) and finding out the differences and parallels between the original balcony scene and this modern pop

(1) Global-to-detailed approach
Introduction: singer, title
▼
First listening
▼
Global comprehension
▼
Second listening
▼
Detailed comprehension
▼
Analysis
(2) PWP approach
Pre-listening activities
▼
While-listening activities
▼
Post-listening activities

Code-referenced approach

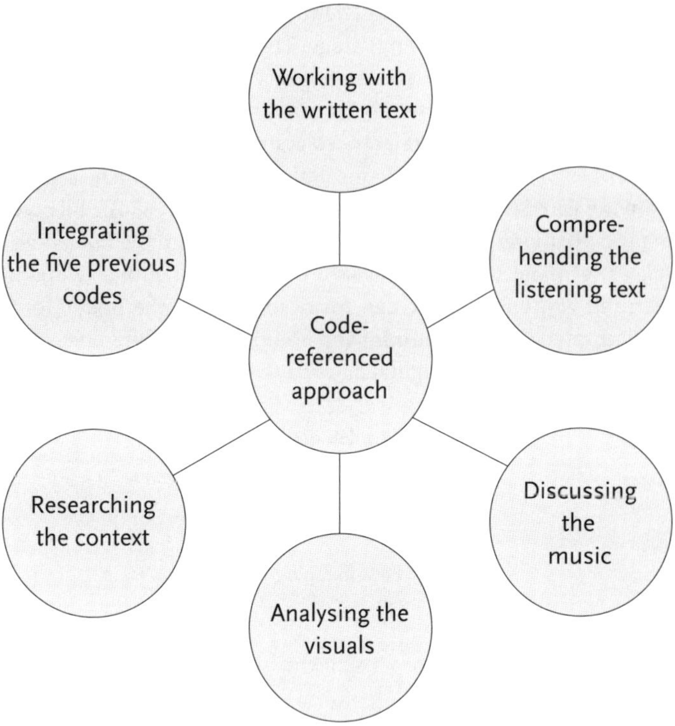

version. Comprehending the listening text may employ the mondegreen technique, i.e. certain words of the lyrics are replaced by mishearings (*Freudsche Verhörer*), and the students have to mark the wrong words on the song sheet and correct them. Discussing the music will lead to the conclusions that lead singer Mark Knopfler talks rather than sings this acoustic track; his blues and country influences are evident, the instrumentation remains simple during the verses, and moves to a full-on rock arrangement only in the chorus sections. If the corresponding music video is available (Dire Straits' *Best of Videos*), the visuals can be analysed and compared with the audio version. As there are a lot of congruences between text and images, a while-viewing task could be to write down all the words that appear both in the lyrics and the video (streetlight, singing, window, dice, to explode, movie, different streets, chains of silver, gold, strangers etc.). Researching the context may lead to the discovery that, apart from the Shakespeare references, the song playfully alludes to other works involving young love, for example the songs *My Boyfriend's Back* and *Somewhere* from the musical *West Side Story*, which is also based on the Verona lovers topos, or that the song was inspired by Mark Knopfler's broken romance with singer Holly Vincent, who, he felt, used him to boost her career, or that this album paved the way for Dire Straits' mainstream success. Integrating the five previous codes seeks to find out how the written, listening, musical, visual, and contextual features complement or contradict each other.

Dire Straits: *Romeo & Juliet* – a mondegreen version

In the following lyrics, one mistake has slipped into every stanza. Identify, mark and correct them.

A lovestruck Romeo sings a streetsuss serenade
Laying everybody low with a love song that he made
Finds a streetlight steps out of the shame
Says something like you and me babe, how about it?

Juliet says hey, it's Romeo, you nearly gimme a heart attack
He's underneath the window she's singing hey la my boyfriend's bag
You shouldn't come around here singing up at people like that
Anyway what you gonna do about it?

Juliet, the ice was loaded from the start
And I bet that you exploded in my arms
And I forget, I forget the movie song
When you gonna realize it was just that the time was wrong Juliet?

Come up on different streets, they both were streets of shame
Both dirty, both mean, yes and the dream was just the same
And I dreamed your dream for you and now your dream is real
How can you look at me as if I was just another one of ordeals?

When you can fall for chains of silver you can fall for chains of gold
You can fall for pretty rangers and the promises they hold
You promised me everything, you promised me thick and thin, yeah
Now you just say oh Romeo, yeah, you know I used to have a scene with him

Juliet, when we made love you used to cry
You said I love you like the stars above, I'll love you till I lie
There's a place for us you know the movie song
When you gonna realize it was just that the time was wrong Juliet?

I can't do the talk like they talk on TV
And I can't do a love song like the way it's meant to be
I can't do everything, but I'd do nothing for you
I can't do anything except be in love with you

And all I do is miss you and the way we used to be
All I do is keep the beat and bad company
Now all I do is risk you through the bars of a rhyme
Juliet, I'd do the stars with you any time

Juliet, when we made love you used to cry ...

A lovestruck Romeo sings a streetsuss serenade ...

Dire Straits. 1980. Making Movies. Straitjacket Songs. Rondor Music, 6359034
(solutions: shade for shame, back for bag, dice for ice, your deals for ordeals, strangers for rangers, die for lie, anything for nothing, kiss for risk)

11.3 Literature & film

When did you watch a film at school? What for?

Benefits of Film Based Language Learning

Film Based Language Learning still leads a kind of Cinderella existence in TEFL classrooms although it can be motivating (remember Andy Warhol's famous aphorism *If it moves they will watch it*), uses authentic material, trains receptive and productive language competences, promotes intercultural as well as media competences and is of high personal relevance – or as literature (and film) expert Helmut Karasek puts it: "There is no biography without the movies" (Thaler 2007a: 10).

4 conflicts – time conflict

This negligence may result from four conflicts. First a film is long, a lesson, however, is short. To integrate 90-minute feature films into TEFL, you therefore have to resort to time-saving approaches of presentation (cf. below) or rely on *independent film study*. One idea here is a *guided movie afternoon*, when teacher and students pay a visit to the local cinema. Prepared during one lesson in class and guided by worksheets with different tasks for pairs, they watch the latest film adaptation and discuss their observation results in the lesson next day. Another idea is *blended film based language learning*, which combines home study (individuals view and study one film of their choice outside class) and classroom work (individual presentation: showing selected scenes and leading the ensuing discussion).

Language conflict

A second conflict results from the linguistic complexity and density of the film on the one hand and the students' restricted language competences on the other. To avoid feelings of frustration students must be encouraged to say farewell to wanting to understand everything. Furthermore the selection of the movie must suit the learners' level – simple plots, congruences between words and pictures, slow and clear RP articulation make viewing-listening comprehension easier. Certain methodological alternatives such as repetitions, segment approach (cf. below), and pre-viewing activities also aid understanding.

Modes of perception conflict

A third conflict, the one between listening and viewing, arises when subtitles are switched on. When both modes of reception are appealed to, "the eye is more powerful than the ear" (Sherman 2001: 16), i.e. viewers tend to focus on the written inserts and neglect listening comprehension. Depending on the teacher's objectives, soundtrack and subtitles can be combined in three different ways: English soundtrack + English subtitles, English soundtrack + mother tongue subtitles, English subtitles + mother-tongue soundtrack. In order to both allow for tuning in to the foreign language and reduce the focus on reading subtitles, the first ten minutes of the film may be shown with the subtitles, and then the subtitles can be switched off.

Goals conflict

A fourth conflict results from diverging goals: teenagers watch movies for entertainment and relaxation, teachers use them to teach and want pupils to learn. "We must be careful to preserve the delicate balance between appreciating a film more because we understand the language, the culture, and the technique behind it, and killing the magic of the experience because we overdo the grammar, the vocabulary, or the pronunciation in the language and comprehension process (Stempleski/Tomalin 2001: 9). To strike this balance between enjoyment and exploitation, teachers are well-advised not to overuse the pause button, the repetition feature, analysis questions, vocabulary work, and grammar worksheets.

4 approaches in FBLL

Having decided on a certain film, the teacher can choose between four modes of presenting it (Thaler 2014). The following table summarizes the advantages and problems (for teachers and learners) of the straight through approach, segment approach, sandwich approach, and clip approach.

Approaches in FBLL

Mode of presentation	*Description*	*Advantages*	*Problems*
Straight through approach	Presentation of the whole film in one sitting, without interruption	– Natural way of watching – Entertainment, suspense, identification, – Little time for preparation	– Danger of passive consumption – Lack of learning efficiency – No *noticing* or *focusing*
Segment approach	Presentation in separate segments (ca. 15'), successive viewing in several lessons	– Combining viewing and working with film – Pre / while / post-viewing tasks in each lesson – Viewing of the entire film	– Cutting up the film – Loss of suspense – Time (6-10 lessons) – Unnatural viewing mode
Sandwich approach	Showing of selected scenes, summarizing deleted scenes (telling)	– Viewing and working – Pre/while/post stages – Less time compared to segment approach – Skipping irrelevant scenes	– Fragmentation and distortion of film – Lack of understanding through incompleteness – More time compared to clip approach
Clip approach	Presentation of one scene / sequence only	– Focus on key scenes (e.g. beginning) – Least time needed – Methodological flexibility – Chance of repeated showing	– Isolation of one scene – Neglecting important aspects – Reduced entertainment and suspense

As for the relationship between literature and film, there are at least five ways in which this can be explored in the classroom: film on book, films on book, book on film, author documentaries, about-literature movies (Thaler 2014). The first and most common way is to use literary adaptations, i.e novels, plays, short stories, even poems turned into short or full-length feature films. As much of classical and also modern literature is now available on video or DVD, reading a book can be supplemented by watching the audio-visual equivalent and comparing the two formats. Such a comparison is meant to identify the parallels and differences, trying to explain why the director decided on the changes he made. However, it should not be guided by a biased preference for the written word, treating the film version as an inferior product. Book and film are two different media with their own aesthetic principles and functions.

5 relations between literature and film – film on book

Very often a book has seen several film adapations by different directors, so a comparison of different films can be a rewarding approach. Each director has his/her own ideas about the aesthetics of a film, settings may vary, actors interpret characters differently, the release date influences production, a certain scene may be emphasized in one film and deleted in another. An effective way, in particular with different versions of Shakespeare, is to choose one important scene and compare the different film adaptations, guided by a grid with several criteria and empty columns for the different films.

films on book

Films are not only produced after a book (*Buchverfilmungen*), but in some cases books are written after a film (*Filmverbuchungen*). Such books on films are not usually of outstanding literary quality, yet they can help us to understand a difficult film. Moreover there are also differences between film and script which can be discussed. The first books on films were Walt Disney's animated cartoons *Robin Hood* and *Cinderella* in the 1950s, and then later written versions of *E.T.*, *Raiders of the Lost Ark*, *The Land Before Time* and *Dead Poets Society* appeared.

Book on film

Another film genre dealing with literature is the *author docu*, i.e. a documentary about the life of a famous author. Such videos or DVDs usually offer insights into the social, political and cultural background of an author's times beyond a mere description of their different life stages, thus contributing to a fuller understanding of their works. For example, Lingua Video

Author docu

has more than 25 bio docus from Austen to Wordsworth in stock.

About literature

Finally there are also some feature films *about* literature. These movies deal with various facets of literature, e.g. the process of writing, the author's problems or the nature of literature. One example is the fantasy comedy *Stranger Than Fiction* (2006), in which the author Karen Eiffel (Emma Thompson) is writing her latest novel about an isolated man named Harold Crick (Will Ferrell). The real Harold leads a dull existence as a taxman, but one day begins to hear Karen's voice as she narrates what she writes down about Harold. Thus the real world (of movie characters) and the literary imagination begin to mingle, and the narration affects Harold's entire life. Another example is Spike Jonze's film *Adaptation* (2002), in which the lovelorn screenwriter Charlie asks his less talented twin brother Donald (both: Nicholas Cage) for help when his efforts to adapt the book *The Orchid Thief* by Susan Orlean (Meryl Streep), which is about the plant dealer John (Chris Cooper), go nowhere. Charlie writes the way he lives – with great difficulty, Donald lives the way he writes – with foolish abandon, Susan writes about life – but can't live it, John's life is a book – waiting to be adapted.

Film analysis

When teachers want to analyse a film, they should draw learners' attention to the specific elements of this genre and their effects, i.e. the cinematic dimension (camera movement, camera angles, camera speed, field sizes, editing, montage, sound, music, colour, lighting), the dramatic dimension (casting, acting, dialogues, locations, props, make-up, costumes), and the literary dimension (story, topics, characters, setting, narrative point of view). As most books on making or teaching films have special chapters or at least glossaries on cinematic devices, they will have no problems getting acquainted with the most important technical terms (Sherman 2001, Stempleski/Tomalin 2003, Thaler 1999, Nünning/Surkamp 2006). Film analysis can be supported by worksheets with illustrations of the various cinematic devices. As well as comprehension and analysis questions, they might include true/false statements, gapped texts, *spot the lie* texts or *who said what* matching exercises.

Open tasks in FBLL

Beyond those traditional and rather closed activities, teachers may select from a number of more open tasks, which leave the students more room for imagination and creation (see table – Thaler 2007a: 13).

Open tasks in FBLL	
Open task	*Description*
Adapting literature	After reading the literary text, students design a storyboard or film script.
Asking the director	After watching a scene, students write down *why* questions for the director. During the second viewing with the voice over commentary by the director, suitable answers are looked for.
Closing the open ending	Students write down unsolved questions concerning the film, which their partners try to answer orally.
Dearest star	Students write a letter to an actor/actress in the film about their impressions.
Debating the issue	A controversy referred to in the film serves as motion for a debate.
Domino	One student writes a key word from the film on the board, the others add further film-related words according to the domino game.
Famous last words	The final scene is frozen (still), and each pupil may speak the *famous last words*.
Film projects	In group work, film projects are developed, e.g. film treatment, film script, film guide, movie magazine, trailer, script. One scene is recorded.
Film response journal	Students keep a diary in which they write down their personal reactions to the film.
Film review	Students write a personal film review and publish it on the Internet – and compare it with other reviews.
Heartstorming	Before viewing students jot down their associations on the title (mind map, word map).
Moving the goal posts	Students ask each other hypothetical questions: *What would happen if (characters/setting ...) were different?*
My favourite scene	Students describe their favourite scene: impact, setting, characters, plot.
Plus – minus – evaluation	Students write positive impressions on the left board, negative ones on the right board, and discuss them.
Predicting the opening	Based on the DVD cover (film poster, photo), students design the opening scene of the film.
Press conference	After viewing, a press conference with actors and director is simulated.

Question pot	Before viewing each student picks one question from a pot, and answers it after viewing.
Remake	Students develop a plan for a remake of a film in a different setting.
Task dice	Each student throws the dice, the number giving them one of six tasks: synopsis, description, quote, imitation, miming, drawing.
Throw the dice	A big dice with six sentence beginnings (I liked ..., I disliked ..., I didn't understand ..., It surprised me ..., The best thing ..., The strangest thing ...) leads to oral statements.
Where are the experts?	Two groups write down quiz questions, which they ask the other group later on.
Wish you were here	Students choose one character from whose perspective they tell the story after viewing.

DVD approaches

Video technology has already broadened the scope of teaching approaches (sound and image manipulation). The DVD, with its language options, subtitles, extras, scene access, has further increased learning opportunities. Those teachers that want to exploit the technical features of DVD (and video) may try out one of the following ideas.

DVD approaches in FBLL

DVD technique	*Description*	*Task (example)*
Normal viewing	Sound on, vision on	*Upside down comprehension*: students answer questions *before* viewing
Silent viewing	Sound off, vision on	Students speculate about the dialogues from what they have seen
Blind listening	Sound on, vision off	Based on what they have heard, students make up a list of objects that may be seen on the video
Freeze frame	Still, pause	Students infer the actors' thoughts and feelings from their frozen images

Split viewing	Half and half: One group watches the video, but does not hear the sound; the other group hears the sound, but does not see the visuals	In pairs students reconstruct the whole situation, filling the information gaps
Jumbled sequence	Several scenes are shown in wrong chronological order	Students reconstruct the correct order and justify it
Fast forward	A film sequence is presented with faster speed	Students give an oral summary of the plot
Rewind	A sequence is presented backwards	Students try to determine cause and effect of storylines
Slow motion	A scene is shown with reduced speed	Students analyse cinematic devices (camera angles and movements, lighting, editing)
English subtitles & English soundtrack	Listening comprehension is supported by subtitles	For tuning into a difficult film, students are given the subtitles during the first 10 minutes
German subtitles & English soundtrack	English dialogues and German subtitles are compared (with the help of the pause button)	Students first write their own German translation of the dialogue, then compare it with the German subtitles
Multi-linguality	Another foreign language apart from English is activated	One scene is watched in English and French (Spanish, Italian) and worked on.
Bonus tracks	Working with the DVD extras (background material)	*Deleted scenes* are evaluated and compared with the book scenes they are based on

11.4 Literature & Internet

Have you ever used the Internet for literature-related purposes?

Using the Internet for literature

The World Wide Web can be used in many ways by teachers and students alike (Thaler 2009b, 2011). You can buy all sorts of books online (e.g. www.amazon.com) after having compared the prices of different booksellers (e.g. www.evenbetter.com). Several websites act as tutors checking your knowledge of literary terms with the help of multiple choice or true / false items (e.g. www.quia.com/quiz/270936.html). There are numerous sites that offer teaching units and lesson plans including author information, plot summaries, character analyses, topics, sample questions, reviews, awards, ideas for using them in the classroom, teaching procedures, and further links (e.g. http://litplans.com, or the British Council's wonderful site http://www.teachingenglish.org.uk/download/britlit/britlit.shtml).

Internet for information

Apart from these functions, the Internet in TEFL is generally used for information, communication, and presentation (or publication).

Internet for information

Technique	*Description*	*Didactic implications*
Web search	Researching the web to find, evaluate and present facts, figures and other data	Rather unguided search; great freedom for students; risk of getting lost in cyberworld
WebQuest	Inquiry-oriented web activity, developed by Bernie Dodge in 1995 (http://webquest.sdsu.edu/); six steps: introduction, task, web sources, description, guidance on presentation, conclusion	Controlled, task-guided exploitation of web information; synthesis between open and closed learning arrangements; focusing on using information rather than looking for it
Web-Unit	Lesson sequences and plans based on coursebook units; accompanied by tasks	Close link to coursebook used in class; e.g. Cornelsen's Web-Units (www.cornelsen-teachweb.de) with teacher module and student module

Web search example: literary puzzle

One example of a *web search* is to ask students to research the life and works of the author whose book is being read, with the aim of writing a *literary puzzle*. This task involves getting an overview of the author's life, selecting key incidents, and writing a personal biography without mentioning his / her name. Read aloud in the classroom or published on the school website or magazine, such a puzzle may trigger intense guessing, lively discussions or written responses.

Another example of a web search aims at finding out who wrote what. Such an *author hunt* is based on a short story which contains a lot of famous books interwoven into the storyline. With the help of the WWW, the students have to identify the corresponding authors (see the beginning of the story *Frieda meets Jura* – Thaler 2006).

2nd example: author hunt

Frieda meets Jura
– a short cross-cultural short story –

Endowed with mind, will and understanding, enough sense and sensibility as well as incendium amoris (the fire of love), Frieda, a lover of English language and literature, set out on a sentimental journey. On the road to east of Eden she stopped to see Jimmy Higgins, Elmer Gantry and a singular man aka Jura, who ran The Hotel New Hampshire in Tobacco Road.

When she arrived, Elmer, the ugly American, who used to work as the deerslayer at Slaughterhouse Five, waved at her wildly and beamed. "Hi honey, welcome to the Monkey House! How's it going in the world according to Garp?" he asked excitedly and looked like the great Gatsby.

"Well, pretty good! It's great to see you guys again. I'm so glad to be back in our gang," she giggled and hugged Elmer and Jimmy each before she asked: "And where's Jura, the playboy of the western world? …

As anyone can print anything on the web, a general problem of web research is that the information may be incomplete, incorrect, dated or completely bogus. That's why it is necessary to give the students websites that the teacher has checked before, and/or to help them learn how to evaluate a website before taking down the information. Students should learn to pay attention to authorship (a reputed institution or a private homepage? sponsor? location – .edu: educational material, .com: commercial material), coverage (topics), accuracy, objectivity, currency, and form.

Evaluating websites

Internet for communication – e-mail

Apart from information, the WWW is an innovative medium for communication. One of the most popular communicative tools that is also used in foreign language classrooms is e-mail. A carefully planned and monitored e-mail project between two schools is an excellent way of increasing pupils' skills in many areas. First, you have to locate a partner school (e.g. http://www.epals.com/) and establish good communication with the teachers there. Together you have to decide on the topic of your joint literary project, as well as your aims, the timing, how to group learners, rules about communication and how to deal with problems. All children should be involved in receiving, creating and sending e-mails, but they will need time to do all that, and teachers have to accommodate different speeds of working and different content. Literary works suitable for class exchanges are, for example, short stories which have a certain thematic complexity, interpretational ambiguity and linguistic density to be able to evoke diverse responses, and which trigger comparisons between the participants' own cultures. For example, Walker's short story *The Flowers* (1973) became the focus of an exchange between German and American students, leading to cultural misunderstandings due to different cultural assumptions (American South, race). The discussions that followed forced both sides to revise their different perspectives (Müller-Hartmann/Schocker-von Ditfurth 2004: 130f.).

Book rap

Another e-mail project that is less time-consuming than a class exchange is the so-called *book rap*. This is a book discussion conducted via electronic mail, in which individuals or groups from around the world can discuss the scheduled books. Teachers can nominate a book for discussion by becoming a book rap coordinator (http://rite.ed.qut.edu.au/old_oz-teachernet/projects/book-rap/).

Internet for communication

Tool	*Description*	*Didactic implications*
E-Mail exchange	Asynchronous, written form of digital communication	Exchange between classes or two partners (tandem) in different countries; strict organization needed
Newsgroup, forum, bulletin board	Virtual notice boards for global asynchronous interaction	Open and closed forms; problems with open forms (participants, topics, language); log files for analysis later on

Chat	Synchronous, written form of communication	User-friendly conferencing tool; hybrid between written and spoken English; simultaneous talk with more people; private topics; multi-threaded discussion
Chatbot	Synchronous, written form of communication with a chat robot	Talking/writing to a cyber person, chat programme, A.I. (Artificial Intelligence), open access, example: ALICE (Artificial Linguistic Internet Computer Entity), natural conversational language
MOO	*Multi-User-Domain Object Oriented*: synchronous, written communication	*Virtual reality*, representations in the form of avatars; complex structure
Video-conferencing	Synchronous communication via sound and image	Meetings between classes from different countries; problem of time coordination; preparation of content and questions necessary
Audio-conferencing	Synchronous communication via sound	Conversation between participants with the aid of headsets; videoconferencing without seeing

Internet for presentation

Finally the Internet can be used for presentation and publication. The prospect of reaching the whole world to extend one's readership is exciting. A good starting point for getting ideas on hypertext projects, i.e. text files with internal links and external links to other texts and sources of information, is Reinhold Donath's website (http://www.englisch.schule.de/reinhard.htm). You can find a lot of hypertexts on literary works produced by pupils from grade 5 to 13, e.g. the detective story *Dead End for Murder* analysed by younger students, a cybernovel called *The Ghost Ship* written by 9th graders and inspired by similar stories in the textbook used in class, several projects by 10th and 11th graders on famous young adult novels (Sachar's *Holes*, Lowry's *The Giver*, O'Brien's *Z for Zachariah*), Billy Joel's song *We Didn't Start the Fire* about 50 years of American culture, or Rowling's *Harry Potter and the Philosopher's Stone*, and finally many projects by 12th and 13th graders on classic novels (Steinbeck's *Of Mice and Men*, Fitzgeralds's *The*

Great Gatsby, Salinger's *The Catcher in the Rye*, Boyle's *Tortilla Curtain*, Auster's *Moon Palace*) and dramas (Shaw's *Pygmalion*, Shakespeare's *Richard III* as well as *Romeo and Juliet*).

Internet for presentation

Technique	*Description*	*Didactic implications*
Homepage	Designing a class, school or student website	Individual, pair or group work; simple homepage generators available (e.g. www.lo-net.de)
Hypertext-Project	Working on a topic with the aim of presenting the results in the form of a hypertext	Project work (planning, carrying out, presenting); using internal and external links;
Weblog (Blog)	Continuous writing of a personal online diary	Website with periodical additions; conclusions from a personal web tour; topical and current version of a newsletter; simple content management systems
Internet video	Recording one's own video and uploading it onto web channels like YouTube	Student-centred, autonomous, process and product-oriented learning

Video sharing websites

Owing to the enormous success of Internet portals like YouTube, the short Internet video has been hailed by some as *the* new medium of our era (cf. Thaler 2008). On the one hand this new trend may be criticised (e.g. for ignoring the border between what is public and what is private, exhibitionism, striving for fame, plagiarism, copyright), on the other, it opens up new possibilities to work creatively with a piece of literature. For example, students' impressions after reading a novel or play can be summarized in one-minute videos, a format which British schools have been experimenting with for quite some time now.

Intermedial Teaching Unit: *Alice in Wonderland*

A teaching unit that makes use of all three media – music, film, Internet – and even more media is based on the reading of Lewis Carroll's *Alice in Wonderland*.

Teaching Unit	
Topic:	*Alice in Wonderland*
Aims:	integrated skills, media and information literacy
Level:	from grade 11
Time:	5 lessons
Procedure:	– 1st lesson: comparing a selected scene from two film adaptations – 2nd lesson: listening and discussing the song *White Rabbit* – 3rd lesson: researching the Internet on the genesis of the book – 4th lesson: listening to and understanding an audio book version – 5th lesson: looking up animal idioms in an English dictionary
Materials:	– *Alice in Wonderland*. Columbia Pictures Television. 1985 – *Alice*. Condor Features Production. 1988 – Jefferson Airplane: *The Masters*. Eagle Records. 1997 (incl. *White Rabbit* by Grace Slick. 1966) – *Alice in Wonderland and Through the Looking Glass*. Audio book, read by Alan Bennett. BBC Young Collection. 1992

Tasks

1. Listen to Dire Straits' song *Romeo & Juliet* and do the following tasks:
   a) Find out the differences and parallels between Shakespeare's balcony scene and Dire Straits' modern pop version.
   b) Add another stanza to the song, consisting of four lines with the rhyme scheme aabb.
2. Cinematic devices:
   The following text summarizes field sizes, camera movements, camera positions and camera angles, including their general effects. Fill in the gapped text with the following cinematic terms:

   bird's eye view – crane shot – establishing shot – extreme close-up – eye-level shot – medium – over-the-shoulder shot – panning – point-of-view shot – shot – static shot – tilting – tracking shot – worm's eye view – zooming

Cinematic devices

Field size refers to the kind and size of shot in a film. A long .... (a) shows people and objects from a distance, giving a complete view of the setting. The whole body or object is presented in a full shot. A .... (b) shot zooms in closer on the actors and shows the upper body or part of an object. Head and shoulders are usually seen in a close-up, which draws the attention to the face, e.g. in order to show emotions. To focus the most important object or part of a face in a scene, a detailed shot or .... (c) is employed.
The simplest form of *camera movement* is the .... (d), when the camera does not move, which evokes a calm and peaceful state. .... (e) means the camera moves from left to right or vice versa, which may give the viewer a feeling of orientation. The camera going up and down is called .... (f), which often increases tension by examining something in greater detail. In a .... (g) the camera is placed on a vehicle moving on the ground. When the camera moves flexibly in all directions high up on a crane, we speak of a .... (h). .... in can focus important details, zooming out discloses the whole context of the situation.
Camera positions comprise, among others, a .... (j), which shows the action through a character's eyes, an .... (k), which shows the location at the start of a scene, and an .... (l), emphasizing the role of the speaker or listener in a dialogue.
Of the three basic *camera angles*, an .... (m) is neutral and undramatic, whereas a high-angle shot (from above), also called .... (n), makes people seem smaller, weak and inferior, and the low-angle shot (from below), also called .... (o), makes people seem bigger, powerful, superior or threatening.

3. Read the cross-cultural short story *Frieda meets Jura* again, discover the titles of famous books hidden in the story, and look for the corresponding authors in the WWW.

12 Assessment

12.1 Standards

Look at the following aphorisms on testing. Which do you like most? Why?

- Not everything that counts can be counted and not everything that can be counted counts. (Albert Einstein)
- In examinations those who do not wish to know ask questions of those who cannot tell. (Sir Walter Raleigh)
- Competence, like truth, beauty and contact lenses, is in the eye of the beholder. (Laurence J. Peter)
- The difference between school and life? In school, you're taught a lesson and then given a test. In life, you're given a test that teaches you a lesson. (Anonymous)
- Rather fail with honour than succeed by fraud. (Sophocles)

Backwash effect

It goes without saying that testing is not very popular with students (Thaler 2012). So the question arises if it is really necessary to test literary competences. Why not reserve a *test-free literature zone*, when all the other aspects of learning are permanently tested anyway? Don't we kill the learners' enjoyment of a good book, if they know they will be examined on it later on? Unfortunately there is a phenomenon called *backwash effect*, which necessitates testing literature as well. According to the backwash (or washback) effect, what is being tested is taught and learned – and, vice versa, what is not being tested, is not learned (and taught). So if we do without literature exams, the value placed on this subject in the learners' minds will decrease, and the need to learn will consequently be felt less.

Functions of testing

Apart from the backwash effect, the literature on assessment mentions further reasons for testing (Thaler 2012). Such general purposes of assessment include:

- selection (*Schule als Lebens-Chancen-Verteilungs-Institution*)
- placement (screening students for certain courses)
- achievement (How far have the students progressed in relation to the goals specified in the curriculum or textbook?)
- proficiency (What do they know in relation to the application of the subject in the real world?)

- feedback for teachers (What have my students not understood yet?)
- feedback for learners (In what fields must I try harder?)
- (external) motivation (I'm going to learn in order to get a good mark)

Classical features of quality

If testing literature is indespensable, it should, however, be done well. Good assessment practice respects the three classical features, i.e. validity, reliability, objectivity, and a number of other characteristics. A test is valid if it really tests what it claims to test. So if our goal is literary communicative competence, and an exam intends to assess the full range of LCC, multiple choice items on literary knowledge are not sufficient. Of the three components of LCC (knowledge, skills, attitudes), the one covering personal attitudes is definitely hardest to evaluate.

A test is reliable, if it produces consistent results even if it is administered on different occasions or by different testers. (Inter-rater and intra-rater) reliability is harder to fulfil the more creative and open a task is. This criterion of quality bears some similarity to objectivity. As there is no such thing as absolute objectivity in assessing a phenomenon as complex as LCC, we should be content if we reach "informed subjectivity to the greatest possible extent" (Klippert, In: Müller-Hartmann/Schocker-von Ditfurth 2004: 149).

Sets of criteria

Reliability and objectivity are easier to achieve if teachers have access to a clear, precise and practical set of criteria which guides them in assessing students' products. The most basic set consists of two criteria, i.e. content and language. For essays on literature, Collie/Slater (1987: 254) have developed a more detailed set consisting of knowledge of the book, essay structure, language, illustration, relevance, coverage, and originality. To evaluate open, creative tasks is even harder than judging essays; Nünning/Surkamp (2006: 59) suggest the following set of criteria:

- length (100 words in grade 5 – 400 words in grade 10)
- reference to task (instructions, completeness)
- thoughts and ideas (quantity, quality)
- composition and coherence (lucidity, plausibility, structure)
- reference to text form (register, addressee, intention, situation)
- form (layout, paragraphs, presentation, appendices)

- language (vocabulary, syntax, connectives, grammar, spelling)

Feasibility

Beyond the three traditional features of good assessment, a few more may be mentioned with regard to literature. Feasibility means that an assessment tool should be practical, as teachers work under time pressure, can see just a portion of students' literary performances and cannot handle a set of 15 different criteria. "Testing is sometimes the art of the possible" (Johnson 2001: 36).

Variety

Variety is another feature. Modern test theory postulates a combination of discrete-point testing, integrative testing and pragmatic testing. Transferred to the field of literature, this means a mixture of testing isolated elements of literature (e.g. literary terms), integrated communicative skills and competences (e.g. composing an essay), and real-life tasks (e.g. writing a review). A test which consists of more parts also appeals to several learner types and does not favour one type only. It can provide different levels of difficulty and thus lead to a differentiation of results (*Trennschärfe*).

Written and oral assessment

Finally teachers should not forget that there are written and oral forms of communication. The priority has traditionally been placed on written tests, as they are said to be more objective. Yet as oral literary competences are also important, they should and can be assessed.

12.2 Test formats

How would you assess LCC?

CEFR: types of assessment

According to the Common European Framework of Reference for Languages (Council of Europe 2001: chapter 9), there are various types of assessment, several of which are also relevant for LCC. A first pair of types is *formative assessment*, i.e. an ongoing process of gathering information on students' progress, and *summative assessment*, i.e. evaluating what students have learned at the end of a course with a grade. A similar pair is called *continuous assessment*, which refers to students' performances throughout the course, and *fixed-point assessment*, which is based on an exam taking place at a particular day. Then a distinction is made between *holistic assessment*, which means making a global synthetic judgement, and *analytical assessment*, looking at different aspects separately and often breaking down evaluation into a set of criteria. Testing literature can also be *criterion-referenced* (the learners are assessed purely in terms of their abilities in literaure) or *norm-referenced* (in relation to their peers in class, rank order, bell curve). Another distinction is made between *assessment by others*, which has been the dominant mode so far with the teacher as *grade-giver*, and *peer* as well as *self-assessment*, which are being proposed in more and more publications.

5 assessment categories of LCC

As LCC covers a lot of different components, including factual knowledge, special skills and appropriate attitudes, the choice of test formats must reflect this wide range. A lot of national guidelines demand the three levels of comprehension, analysis, and evaluation. The nature of LCC suggests a refinement and expansion to comprise the following five categories.

Assessing LCC

Category	*Examples*
Comprehension	• Content questions • Excerpt-based questions • Summary • True-false statements • Matching exercises • Multiple choice items • Gapped text • Odd one out exercise • Error spotting etc.
Analysis	• Questions • Paraphrasing • Applying literary terminology etc.
Evaluation	• Comment • Review • Essay • Book report etc.
Creation	• Creative writing • Visual, auditory, audio-visual, interactive forms • Scenic presentation (performing a play etc.)

Process orientation	• Portfolio • Reading journal • Self-evaluation sheets etc.

6-step approach to answering questions

The last category in particular may also give information on students' attitudes to literature, which are always difficult to pin down. So far, a majority of classroom tests, however, have been based on comprehension questions, i.e. whether one has understood the content of a text. To improve this basic skill, teachers should help students get accustomed to the six-step approach as the standard procedure of answering questions in written form (Thaler 2007c: 287).

Answering questions on a text

Step 1: *Reflecting*

Read the question carefully. A lot of wrong answers result from misunderstanding or just partly understanding what is asked.

▼

Step 2: *Scanning*

Look for the passage or passages in the text that provide information on the question. Sometimes the passages are scattered throughout the text, so do not be content with having found a single passage.

▼

Step 3: *Marking*

Underline or highlight the relevant questions. Put the number of the question in the margin (to avoid confusions with other questions).

▼

Step 4: *Reducing*

Determine the key items of the passages marked. Are there any repetitions or redundancies? What are the essential points? Put the items into a logical order. You can underline the key items, or jot them down on a separate sheet.

▼

Step 5: *Writing*

- Answer in complete, coherent sentences.
- The first sentence answers the question in general, the following sentences support your analysis.
- If the question consists of more parts, answer them in the order given.
- Do not copy from the text, but use your own words as far as possible.
- Use present tense (unless question requires past).
- Vary the syntax, use connectives, avoid repetitions and waffling.
- Use neutral style (no colloquialisms, no slang, no short forms).
- If you do not know a word, paraphrase it (do not leave a gap).
- For quotations use quotation marks (both are on top). Avoid long ones.
- Do not mix textual analysis with personal opinion.

Useful connectives: according to the text ... it is written ... the author says ...
firstly ... secondly ... thirdly ...
furthermore ... besides ... then ... moreover ... similarly ... but above all ...
yet ... despite ... although ... in contrast to ... contrary to ...
it may be true that ... but ..., on the one hand ... on the other ...
as ... therefore ... due to ... because of ...

▼

Step 6: *Editing*
Read your answer and check it. Have you covered all content aspects? Is the language correct?

Reading logs

Apart from the rather conventional test formats, more student-centred ways of evaluation have been recommended in recent years, like logs, portfolios or peer assessment. A reading log (book journal) is a written dialogue with a fictional text. Writing down one's personal responses to a novel or drama makes one think about what is being read. It helps students to gain insight about the theme and plot, to find out about their feelings with the characters, they remember better what they have read, and they may expand their overall enjoyment of literature. It must be admitted though that many students are not too keen on pursuing the time-consuming task of regularly writing in entries about their personal reactions. If they can be convinced, they just need a notebook (or an exercise book), which is divided into three columns (two big ones and a small one). Then they must be encouraged to make their entries after each chapter or at other appropriate moments while reading (Thaler 2007c: 290ff.).

How to keep a reading log

First column	*Second column*	*Third column*
• Write down facts needed for class discussion or tests. • Think of plot, structure, setting, characters, point of view, style. • Quote from the text (use dots for showing what is left out).	• State your personal reactions. • You may use telegram style. • What feelings does the book/paragraph invoke? • Are there any connections between the fictional text and your life?	• Use special signs (in different colours) here. • They tell you to look up words in dictionaries and encyclopedias. • They remind you to ask class members about points which are not clear.

• Add the page number for quicker reference later on.	• Would you like to be one of the characters? Why (not)? • Stop after a paragraph and guess how the story might develop.	

Process view of assessment

To conclude, it must be emphasized that testing and assessment should be seen as a process. Everything stated so far on standards and test formats refers to just one, i.e. the second stage – out of five stages:

1. preparation
2. design
3. administration
4. correction
5. feedback

A process view makes clear that students deserve a goal-oriented preparation, which informs them about the requirements and practises the relevant test formats in advance. The test is designed according to accepted criteria of quality and using appropriate formats. Administering a test has to guarantee fair conditions and an agreeable working atmosphere – the instructions in the failure manual (see table) should not be taken at face value. Correcting should be done in a transparent and fair manner, using credits or grades, and pave the way for personal feedback, which shows the students both their weak and strong points and motivates them to carry on reading.

How to fail your literature exam
• Bring a pillow. Fall asleep (or pretend to) until the last 15 minutes. Wake up, say "oh geez, better get cracking" and do some gibberish work. Turn it in a few minutes early. • Get a copy of the exam, run out screaming "Andre, Andre, I've got the secret documents!" • Make paper airplanes out of the exam. Aim them at the teacher's left nostril. • Talk the entire way through the exam. Read questions aloud, debate your answers with yourself out loud. • Walk in, get the exam, sit down. About five minutes into it, loudly say to the teacher, "I don't understand ANY of this. I've been to every literature class. What's the deal? And who the hell are you? Where's the regular guy?"

- On the answer sheet find a new, interesting way to refuse to answer every question. For example: "I refuse to answer this question on the grounds that it conflicts with my religious beliefs." Be creative.
- Do the entire exam in another language. If you don't know one, make one up!
- Leave the classroom sneering at the teacher: "I hate literature anyway!"

adapted from: http://www.crazystudent.com/exams/tips/fail.htm

12.3 Course assessment

What have you learned from this book?

University courses

University teachers, who have used this book in their course and need to assess their students, may take a few ideas from the assessment I have used with my students at the University of Education Freiburg. The final grade of my second- and third-term students, who attended the seminar "Introduction to Teaching English Literature" (14 weeks, 90 minutes per week), was based on three requirements: participation, portfolio, and final exam.

Requirements

Unless the number of students renders any evaluation of students' participation impossible, their oral contributions during the weekly meetings may be evaluated via holistic assessment (20 % of final grade). For their portfolio they had to complete five tasks: writing a short book report, inventing a literary quiz on an author, compiling a *bluffer's guide* to a book they know, creating a mini-saga, justifying the inclusion of a certain novel into the Alternative Top Ten. The folder was evaluated via analytical assessment, using a set of criteria like completeness, content, argumentation, language competence, form (40 % of final grade). In the last term week, students had to do a final exam, which tested, on the one hand, their knowledge of the course contents, and, on the other, their understanding of a novel they all had to read during the term (Frank McCourt: *Teacher Man*). The test lasted 60 minutes, consisted of different questions and attributed credits to each of them (40 % of final grade).

Final exam

The questions of this final exam are presented in the following table.

Final exam

Introduction to the Teaching of Literature

Maximum number of points: 70 Your score: ...... Your grade: ......
Name: .... *Good luck!*

Part I: General knowledge

1. Rationale *5 cr.*
List five reasons why we should teach literature in our English classes.

2. Reading *8 cr.*
a) Which of the three models of the reading process do you favour? Explain briefly.
b) Name three reasons why we should encourage silent reading in our English classes.

3. Literary theory *4 cr.*
Find the approaches to literary theory matching the following definitions.

approach	*short definition*
	looking at works on the basis of what is written, not at the author's biography
	emphasizing themes of class conflict, exploitation
	examining a text by also studying other texts of the same time period
	focusing upon the active reaction of the reader to a text

4. Procedures for text work *4 cr.*
Ranking, reduction, and reconstruction are three procedures of text work (Maley/Duff). Choose one and argue why you prefer this procedure with short narrative forms.

5. Clerihews *4 cr.*
Are you going to use clerihews in your future English classes? Explain why (not).

6. Literary terms *11 cr.*
a) Complete this grid by filling in the corresponding terms or definitions.

literary term	*definition*
pun	
	last part of a play after the climax, in which the conflict is solved
tragedy	
	verbal and dramatic hints suggesting what is to come later
	a character does not perceive what his fate holds in store, but the spectator knows better
simile	

b) Which literary terms do the following lines exemplify?
- ....: *rest room* instead of *toilet*
- ....: Love's fire heats water, water cools not love.
- ....: Where will we three wander hither?
- ....: Life's but a poor player that struts and frets his hour upon the stage

7. Lesson planning *12 cr.*
Choose one poem and design a brief lesson plan (45 minutes) for an intermediate class. Also state briefly what your main objectives for this lesson are.

Part II: Understanding McCourt's Teacher Man

8. Point of view *5 cr.*
What point of view is this novel written from? What consequences does that have for the relationship to the reader?

9. Setting *3 cr.*
Describe the setting of the last part briefly.

10. Ending *3 cr.*
The last chapter of the book only consists of the words "I'll try". Explain why.

11. Diction *3 cr.*
Choose three different adjectives to characterize the author's way of writing.

12. TEFL value *8 cr.*
Discuss whether this book is suitable reading material for one of your future classes.

Tasks

1. What's wrong with these test formats here?
   - Mr Nice bases his pupils' literature grades solely on self evaluation and peer assessment. By doing so, he hopes to foster independence and cooperation as well as improve the rapport between pupils and teacher.
   - Ms Discrete prefers gap-filling exercises, cloze passages, sentence transformations, matching exercises, questions, multiple choice formats, and true/false statements in her tests because they are reliable, objective, feasible and practical.
   - Mr Sum prefers the straight through approach to reading plays, novels or short stories, and usually has his students write a summary of the plot before discussion on the book in class begins.

2. Fixed point assessment or continuous assessment: What are their advantages and drawbacks?
3. Try to answer the questions in the final exam (12.3).

Suggested answers for the tasks

Chapter 1

Task 1

Literature with a capital *L*	literature with a small *l*
– Shakespeare drama – Dickens novel – Beckett play – Wordsworth poem – Hemingway short story – Bukovsky poem ?	– pop song lyrics – sketch – graffiti – limerick – joke – anecdote – simplified/graded reader – young adult fiction (?) – hard-boiled detective story – Bukovsky poem ?

Task 2

- sonnet: *Sonnet 18* by William Shakespeare
- ode: *Ode on a Grecian Urn* by John Keats
- limerick: *Book of Nonsense* by Edward Lear
- free verse: *Leaves of Grass* by Walt Whitman
- novel: *England, England* by Julian Barnes
- short story: *You Were Perfectly Fine* by Dorothy Parker
- fable: *The Very Proper Gander* by James Thurber
- anecdote: *My Most Embarrassing Moment* series in Reader's Digest
- tragedy: *Hamlet* by William Shakespeare
- comedy: *Educating Rita* by Willy Russell
- history play: *Richard II* by William Shakespeare
- sketch: *Dead Parrot* by Monty Python

Task 3

Individual answers are expected. One could take one of the Young Adult Novels (e.g. *The Giver* by Lois Lowry) and apply all the 22 criteria, or at least pick one from each of the four groups.

Chapter 2

Task 1

Individual answers are expected. You may choose a play (Arthur Miller's *Death of a Salesman*) or novel (Aldous Huxley's *Brave New World*), which you read during your own school years, and check in retrospect whether it was suitable for your class by applying the various criteria of selection.

Task 2

In primary school, the teacher could tell the story in a few simple sentences, illustrated by a map and followed up by some activity-based treasure hunt (storytelling). In intermediate classes, a graded or simplified reader can be used. Advanced students read the original text (with annotations) and watch one of the film adaptations on DVD.

Task 3

Project Gutenberg, founded in 1996, is a member of The World Electronic Book Library Consortia, which is the world's largest eBook provider. Its aim is to preserve and disseminate classic works of literature, bibliographies, serials, and reference works in a number of languages and countries around the world. Their mission, among others, is to aid students and educators by providing both free public access and an enhanced membership section to the world's most complete collection of electronic texts, books, and documents on-line.

Task 4

- grammatical competence: students learn new words (examples of teachers' and learners' roles)
- discourse competence: students can be made aware of coherence and cohesion in the text achieved by answering questions, giving examples, elaborating on a key item in the subsequent paragraph etc.
- socio-cultural competence: students' attention is drawn to the stylistic differences between an Irish-born, adult teacher and young pupils from lower social classes.
- strategic competence: coping strategies may be trained by having students paraphrase difficult words like 'cocoon'.

Chapter 3

Task 1

50 €: Answer D – Moby Dick
100 €: Answer B – Once upon a time
200 €: Answer D – Agatha Christie
300 €: Answer A – As You Like It

500 €: Answer A – Enid Blyton
1,000 €: Answer C – author
2,000 €: Answer B – Waiting for Godot
4,000 €: Answer B – suicide
8,000 €: Answer B – poem
16,000 €: Answer C – Tolkien
32,000 €: Answer A – F.S. Fitzgerald
64,000 €: Answer A – Cyrano de Bergerac
125,000 €: Answer A – Montague and Capulet
500,000 €: Answer – A – American Psycho
1,000,000 €: Answer B – Uriah Heep

Task 2

Professor Kristi Siegel provides an excellent overview of modern literary theory including comprehensible explanations of the key concepts given at her website: www.kristisiegel.com/theory.htm.

Chapter 4

Task 1

Betty violates the following *commandments*:
She does not like reading ↔ no. 5 and 1
She only reads when told so ↔ no. 1 and 5
She has not got a purpose when reading ↔ no. 6
She looks up every new word ↔ no. 10
She does not read in chunks ↔ no. 4
She makes no use of anticipation ↔ no. 2
She subvocalizes, fixes every word and jumps back ↔ no. 4
She does not make use of prior knowledge ↔ no. 3

Task 2

Step 1: Writing the title on the board and having students speculate about the content
Step 2: First reading – silent reading
Step 3: Global comprehension – checking on whether the students' predictions were correct
Step 4: Second reading – teachers' recitation, several readings by students

Step 5: Detailed comprehension – explaining unknown words, eliciting information on place names (sites of wars)

Step 6: Analysis

a) form: identifiying the poetic form (free verse) and elements of coherence (identity of voice and situation, repetitions, variations, parallelisms, anaphorae), recognizing the speaker and the personification (grass)
b) intention: reflecting on the selection of place names (different times and continents: war and suffering as universal phenomenon), ambiguity of the symbol (people's oblivion and inability to learn from catastrophes, vitality of life)
c) transfer: commenting on Santayana's aphorism: "Those who cannot remember the past are condemned to repeat it."

Task 3
Margaret Atwood: Happy Endings

A.
John and Mary fall in love and get married. They both have worthwhile and remunerative jobs which they find stimulating and challenging. They buy a charming house. Real estate values go up. Eventually, when they can afford live-in help, they have two children, to whom they are devoted. The children turn out well. John and Mary have a stimulating and challenging sex life and worthwhile friends. They go on fun vacations together. They retire. They both have hobbies which they find stimulating and challenging. Eventually they die. This is the end of the story.
C.
John, who is an older man, falls in love with Mary, and Mary, who is only twenty-two, feels sorry for him because he's worried about his hair falling out. She sleeps with him even though she's not in love with him. She met him at work. She's in love with someone called James, who is twenty-two also and not yet ready to settle down.
John on the contrary settled down long ago: this is what is bothering him. John has a steady, respectable job and is getting ahead in his field, but Mary isn't impressed by him, she's impressed by

James, who has a motorcycle and a fabulous record collection. But James is often away on his motorcycle, being free. Freedom isn't the same for girls, so in the meantime Mary spends Thursday evenings with John. Thursdays are the only days John can get away. John is married to a woman called Madge and they have two children, a charming house which they bought just before the real estate values went up, and hobbies which they find stimulating and challenging, when they have the time. John tells Mary how important she is to him, but of course he can't leave his wife because a commitment is a commitment. He goes on about this more than is necessary and Mary finds it boring, but older men can keep it up longer so on the whole she has a fairly good time. .....

The end of the whole story:
... You'll have to face it, the endings are the same however you slice it. Don't be deluded by any other endings, they're all fake, either deliberately fake, with malicious intent to deceive, or just motivated by excessive optimism if not by downright sentimentality. The only authentic ending is the one provided here: John and Mary die. John and Mary die. John and Mary die.
So much for endings. Beginnings are always more fun. True connoisseurs, however, are known to favor the stretch in between, since it's the hardest to do anything with.
That's about all that can be said for plots, which anyway are just one thing after another, a what and a what and a what.
Now try How and Why.

Full story (with options A – F): http://users.ipfw.edu/ruflethe/endings.htm

Chapter 5

Task 1

a) In order to make students read, teachers must be role models and read a lot themselves.
b) If you have not got the opportunity to live in the target country (best way), you should do a lot of extensive reading.
c) You cannot force students to read, they must start liking it.
d) The teacher's task is to provide the proper conditions so that students enjoy reading and want to read more.
e) Only by reading a lot will students become good readers.

Task 2

Individual answers are expected.

Task 3

Possible reasons for commercial success of various bestsellers:
- inclusion of crime and violence appeals to deep-seated primitive instincts
- sex sells
- we need heroes and leader figures to identify with
- the good guy wins, the bad guys are punished, satisfying our sense of justice
- escape literature: the dreariness of everyday life is left behind
- marketing: huge PR budget
- .....

Task 4

Individual answers are expected.

Chapter 6

Task 1

Authentic student's answer (Carola Mayer, 2007):
Being ill
Many symptoms. Feeling miserable. Sore throat. Terrible headache. Clogged sinuses. Runny nose. Bothering mucus. Watery eyes. Aching muscles. Chesty cough. Little energy. High temperature. Sweating frequently. Freezing constantly. No appetite. Going to the doctor. Collecting prescription. Taking medication. Drinking plenty. Eating hot chicken soup. Sleeping a lot. Feeling better gradually.

Task 2

Kongratulations, icecube

Task 3

Six features of a short story and Parker's story:
- incident: a young man's undesired commitment

- plot: dialogue about the man's misbehaviour the previous night, "Ah, now Peter! ..." as turning point and surprising reversal (before: behaviour towards others – now: behaviour towards her is revealed)
- characters: young man and woman, man's double fall: abominable behaviour and undesired commitment (crisis, clash of characters)
- setting: a few minutes in one room, flashback to the night before
- language: double irony of title, repetition of man's first line ("Oh, dear ...) at the end (beginning: physiological consequences – end: psychological and moral consequences)
- suspense: how did he behave? What did he say to the girl? Dénouement: he committed himself more than he meant to

Task 4

Individual presentations are expected.

Chapter 7

Task 1

Authentic student's answer (Julia Brodbeck, 2007):
Joyce Carol Oates: *Big Mouth & Ugly Girl*
In Oates' novel, Matt, the protagonist, tells his friends in school for fun about blowing up the school. Immediately he is suspected of planning an assassination and is therefore suspended from school. There is only one girl that believes him – and she's just the one he never would have thought of.
It is a fantastic book to be used in secondary school. It covers an important current topic and includes a sensitive love story. The language is easy to understand and the narrative mode is varied including emails.

Task 2

1 j, 2 g, 3 h, 4 k, 5 d, 6 a, 7 c, 8 b, 9 f, 10 l, 11 e, 12 i

Task 3

a) text b) passages c) grid d) education e) dynamic – round f) conclusion g) relationships h) quoting j) language

Task 4

- having students predict the content from the cover of the book
- asking them why they (do not) keep a diary
- encouraging them to tell anecdotes about New Year's Eve and 1st January
- making them write eight New Year's resolutions

Task 5

a) foil b) diction c) register d) plot e) story line f) stretch g) iterative mode h) repetitive mode i) discourse j) in medias res k) covert narrator l) unreliable narrator m) deus ex machina

Chapter 8

Task 1 & 2

Individual answers are expected.

Task 3

a) spoonerisms corrected:
"You have missed all my history lectures, and were caught lighting a fire." – angry address to students
"Pardon me madam, this pew is occupied." – excuse in a church
"Let us raise our glasses to the dear old Queen." – toast to Queen Mum
b) Individual answers are expected.
c) misspelt poem corrected: *Spelling chequer*
I have a spelling chequer
It came with my PC
It plainly marks for my review
Mistakes I cannot see.

I strike a key and type a word
And wait for it to say

Whether I am wrong or right
It shows me straight away.

As soon as a mistake is made
It knows before too long
And I can put the error right
It's rarely ever wrong.

I have run this poem through it
I am sure you're pleased to know
It's letter perfect all the way
My chequer told me so.

Task 4

a) repetition: alien
b) anaphora: I'm an alien, I'm a legal alien
c) parallelism: Confront your enemies, avoid them
d) allusion: If "manners maketh man"
e) internal rhyme: modesty, propriety can lead to notoriety
f) ellipsis: Takes more than combat gear to make a man
g) antithesis: confront – avoid

Task 5

x = unstressed syllable, X = stressed syllable, / = pause

x X x x X x x X /	1 iamb, 2 anapaests, 3 beats, pause
x X x x X x x X /	1 iamb, 2 anapaests, 3 beats, pause
x x X x x X /	2 anapaests, 2 beats, pause
x x X x x X /	2 anapaests, 2 beats, pause
x X x x X x x X /	1 iamb, 2 anapaests, 3 beats, end-stopped line

Task 6

10h, 9g, 8f, 7e, 6b, 5a, 4i, 3j, 2d, 1c

Chapter 9

Task 1

a) No. 1: In this award-winning sketch from *Little Britain*, Andy, who pretends to need carer Lou's aid to get around, gets out of his wheelchair and jumps off the highest diving board. Meanwhile an unwitting Lou tells a lifeguard that Andy will need help getting into the water.

b) – YouTube: www.youtube.com/watch?v=YcJfY3e6E6w
– Television: *Little Britain*, Series 1, Episode 1, Title 12, originally aired in 2003, repeated on several channels
– DVD: *Little Britain*, Series 1

c) yes: status as No. 1 sketch, politically incorrect humour, hilarious situation, funny characters
no: politically incorrect portrayal of minority (physically handicapped people), Lou's fast and lisping articulation: hard to understand

Task 2

Solution to crossword puzzle:

			[1]A	C	[2]T							
					U							
[3]C	O	M	I	C	R	E	L	I	E	F		
[4]F	R	O	Z	E	N	T	A	B	L	E	A	U
			[5]S	K	I	T						
[6]S	E	T	T	I	N	G						
					G				[7]C			
		[8]P			[9]P	L	A	Y	L	E	T	
		[10]R	E	S	O	L	U	T	I	O	N	
		O			I				M			
		P			N				A			
		S			T				X			

Task 3

Error in the last paragraph: The Theatre of the ABSURD instead of *Absolute*

Task 4

- Maley/Duff (1982): creative drama techniques, various forms (warmers and coolers, observing, interpreting, creating, problem solving, word play, literary texts)
- Ladousse (1987): various forms of role plays (communication, decision-making, improvising etc.), each with notes on level, aim, time, language, organization, preparation, warm up, procedure, and in particular wonderful role cards
- Wessels (1987): practical advice on how to improve course-book presentation, to teach spoken communication skills, to set up a drama project outside the classroom (from initial improvisations to final performance)
- Scheller (1981): focus on roles (taking roles, making roles, swapping roles, altering roles, double roles), monologue, aside, auto drama etc.
- Meyer (1997): learning by teaching, students as directors and actors, staging Shakespeare's *A Midsummer Night's Dream*
- Wilkening (1998): drama techniques in open, student-centred arrangements, first year (*class magnet picture*), 3rd year (fairy tale), 4th year (Western), advanced classes (short absurd dramas)
- Bludau (2000): poem as stimulus for pantomime, designing a script with cue cards, *Macbeth*: writing a script and staging it

Chapter 10

Task 1 & 2

Individual answers are expected.

Tasks 3

a) Students' speculations: a beautiful young woman (Sonnet 18), an ugly but good-hearted woman the speaker loves (Sonnet 130) – Sonnet 18 is not addressed to the mysterious "dark lady", and probably not to a young man ("the fair youth"), as is often thought – "this" and "thee" in the heroic couplet of Sonnet 18 refer to the sonnet itself: the sonnet or poetry in general are glorified

b) 14 lines, three stanzas of four lines (quatrains) and one stanza of two lines (heroic couplet): typical English/Shakespearian sonnet form with the main message in the final couplet, rhyming scheme: abab cdcd efef gg

c) Sonnet 18: Shakespeare praises the sonnet as a divine form of poetry and idolization of a beloved person.
Sonnet 130: This sonnet constitutes an elaborate parody on the conventions of Petrarchan love poetry common during Shakespeare's time.

Task 4

Woman's soliloquy
To hate or not to hate; that is the question;
Whether it is nobler to hold our words in
At the person that boils our blood
Or just let it all go
And by opposing they will win. To calm down; to relax;
No more; and by not relaxing, I mean to fight
Losing my energy when he bothers not to move.
Losing my voice when he bothers not to listen
My breath wasted at an ignorant person
Due to the fact that he wants to win.
To calm down, to relax;
To relax: Perchance to catch my breath
And think carefully in a plot that I may win
Aye, there's the ring.
And to that desperately needed break there comes a time to think.
When I have yelled and screamed my lungs out
He must give in and there is my reward
That makes losing my voice worth it.

Amelia Handoyo (slightly adapted)

Chapter 11

Task 1

a) Differences and parallels between the two texts:

Differences		
	Shakespeare	Dire Straits
genre	play, tragedy	pop song, lyrics, ballad

point of view	dialogue, Romeo and Juliet taking turns at talking	third person point of view, alternately Romeo's and Juliet's perspective
length	> 100 lines	~ 40 verses
setting	medieval Verona	modern-day city (with movies)
plot background	Montagues vs Capulets	no family feud mentioned, other love relationships (l. 17-21)
language	early modern English	colloquial, spoken, modern English
concept of love	beginning of love, romantic notion, erotic overtones, words as a medium of love	looking back on love (gone? l. 12), singing songs as an instrument of love (l. 2)
Parallels: names (Romeo, Juliet), love relationship, place (l. 6: "underneath the window"), promise of eternal love		

b) I just can't dress up like they do on a catwalk
And I don't wanna be like TV men who just talk and talk
I may be a fool, but I really love you
Tell me, do you love me, too?

Task 2

Cinematic devices: (a) shot (b) medium (c) extreme close-up (d) static shot (e) Panning (f) tilting (g) tracking shot (h) crane shot (i) Zooming (j) point-of-view shot (k) establishing shot (l) over-the-shoulder shot (m) eye-level shot (n) bird's eye view (o) worm's eye view

Task 3

Works and authors in *Frieda meets Jura*:
- *Mind, Will and Understanding*: Anonymous/Macro Plays (ca. 1425)

– *Sense and Sensibility*: Jane Austen (1811)
– *Incendium Amoris (The Fire of Love)*: Richard Rolle (ca. 1340)
– *A Sentimental Journey*: Laurence Sterne (1768)
– *On the Road*: Jack Kerouac (1957)
– *East of Eden*: John Steinbeck (1952)
– *Jimmy Higgins*: Upton Sinclair (1919)
– *Elmer Gantry*: Sinclair Lewis (1927)
– *A Singular Man*: J.P. Donleavy (1963)
– *The Hotel New Hampshire*: John Irving (1981)
– *Tobacco Road*: Erskine Caldwell (1932)
– *The Ugly American*: William J. Lederer & Eugene Burdick (1958)
– *The Deerslayer*: James F. Cooper (1841)
– *Slaughterhouse Five*: Kurt Vonnegut (1968)
– *Welcome to the Monkey House*: Kurt Vonnegut (1968)
– *The World According to Garp*: John Irving (1978)
– *The Great Gatsby*: F. Scott Fitzgerald (1925)
– *Our Gang*: Philip Roth (1971)
– *The Playboy of the Western World*: J.M. Synge (1907)

Chapter 12

Task 1

– Mr Nice does not see the danger of students assessing themselves or peers too positively, self and peer assessment should be complemented by teacher assessment.
– Ms Discrete favours discrete-point testing, neglects integrative and pragmatic testing, cannot cover all aspects of LCC (skills, attitudes?).
– Mr Sum ignores the criterion of variety; his tests consist of just one part.

Task 2

Fixed point assessment:
+ long-established tradition, transparent, traditional criteria of quality (validity, reliability, objectivity) can be met
– may lead to examination traumas, favours certain types of learners

Continuous assessment:
+ is not dependent on a single performance, covers a long period, creativity can be taken account of, different strengths are considered

– depends on the teacher's capacity to be objective, bureaucratic nightmare for the teacher, school life as a never-ending test for the learner

Task 3

(1) language development, intercultural learning, personal enrichment, motivational value, interpretational openness (+ social prestige)
(2) a) one of the three models, preferably interactive one: short description and argumentation required (synthesis of bottom-up and top-down)
b) natural way of reading, fast mode, deeper understanding
(3) New Criticism, (Neo-) Marxism, New Historicism, Reader Response
(4) individual answers, e.g. reduction: the length of the text is reduced by deleting words or sentences requirements: close reading, understanding, focus on key points
(5) definition of clerihew, mentioning pros (short, funny, rhyme, famous persons, suitable for creative writing) or cons (rather unknown genre, humour as a matter of taste, difficult to find suitable persons or rhyming words)
(6) a) play on words, dénouement, serious drama in which the tragic hero suffers a tragic fate (tragic flaw), foreshadowing, dramatic irony, comparison with 'like' or 'as'
b) euphemism, chiasmus, alliteration, personification
(7) individual answers: a few suggestions for pre-, while-, post stages, stating some objectives (language awareness, creative writing etc.)
(8) first-person, protagonist-narrator, limited point of view close relationship to reader, chance of identification with autobiographical writer
(9) author's (and narrator's) last (and best) stage in his life as a teacher, Stuyvesant High in New York, late 20th century
(10) reference to ending of preceding chapter, narrator's reaction to student's suggestion of writing a book
(11) humorous (ironical), personal, colloquial – condescending, boastful, repetitive
(12) 'discuss' means both pros and cons:
– pros: familiar setting and topics (school), students'

identification with McCourt's students, not difficult to understand, humorous style, renowned author
– cons: teacher's point of view (not students'), strands of authorial self-love and self-justification, story becoming weaker in the second part of the book

Bibliography

A

Antor, H. (ed.) *Shakespeare alternativ.*
1997 | Themenheft Der Fremdsprachliche Unterricht Englisch, 6/1997

B

Bachtin, M. *Die Ästhetik des Wortes.*
1979 | Frankfurt a.M.: Suhrkamp

Bergmann, B. Kroth, O. (ed.) *Shakespeare creative.*
2002 | Themenheft Der Fremdsprachliche Unterricht Englisch, 2/2002

Beyer-Kessling, V. *Put it in writing. Kreatives Schreiben im Englischunterricht der Sekundarstufe.*
2002 | In: Fremdsprachenunterricht 46/2002, pp. 334 – 339

Bieri, P. *Wie sollen wir leben?*
2007 | In: ZEITmagazin 32/2007, pp. 26 – 27

Biermann, W. *Das ist die feinste Liebeskunst. 12 Shakespeare-Sonette.*
2005 | In: CD, Berlin: Zweitausendeins

Bludau, M. *Szenisches Spielen – ein Weg zu ganzheitlichem Sprachhandeln.*
2000 | In: Fremdsprachenunterricht 1/2000, pp. 15 – 21

Bludau, M. *Übendes Schreiben im Englischunterricht der Sekundarstufe I.*
1998 | In: Fremdsprachenunterricht 51/1998, pp. 11 – 17

Booth, D. et al. *Choosing Children's Books.*
1987 | Markham: Pembroke

Bredella, W. *Literarisches und interkulturelles Verstehen*
2002 | Tübingen: Narr

Bushman, J. Bushman, K. *Using Young Adult Literature in the English Classroom.*
1997 | Englewood Cliffs: Prentice Hall

Byram, Michael *Teaching and Assessing Intercultural Communicative Competence.*
1997 | Clevedon: Multilingual Matters

C

CASPARI, D. *Kreativität im Umgang mit literarischen Texten im Fremdsprachenunterricht.* 1994 | Frankfurt a.M.: Lang

COPE, B. KALANTZIS, M. *Multiliteracies: Literacy Learning and the Design of Social Futures* 2000 | London: Routledge

COLLIE, J. SLATER, S. *Literature in the Language Classroom.* 1987 | Cambridge: Cambridge University Press

COODY, B. *Using Literature with Young Children.* 1997 | Madison: Brown and Benchmark

COUNCIL OF EUROPE (ED.) *Common European Framework of Reference for Languages.* 2001 | Cambridge: Cambridge University Press, www.coe.int/t/dg4/linguistic/CADRE_EN.asp

D

DAY, R. BAMFORD, J. *Extensive Reading in the Second Language Classroom.* 1998 | Cambridge: Cambridge University Press

DELANOY, W. *Fremdsprachlicher Literaturunterricht.* 2002 | Tübingen: Narr

DUFF, A. MALEY, A. *Literature.* 1990 | Oxford: Oxford University Press

DUXBURY, J. *Shakespeare Meets the Backbeat: Literary Allusions in Rock Music.* 1988 | In: Popular Music & Society 12-3/1988, pp. 19 – 23

E

ELLIS, G. BREWSTER, J. *Tell it Again! The New Storytelling Handbook for Primary Teachers* 2002 | London: Penguin

ELLIS, G. MCRAE, J. *The Extensive Reading Handbook for Secondary Teachers* 1991 | London: Penguin

F

FAULSTICH, W. *Rock – Pop – Beat – Folk. Grundlagen der Textmusikanalye.* 1978 | Tübingen: Narr

Froese, W. *Kreatives Schreiben im Englischunterricht der Sekundarstufe I.*
1999 | In: Fremdsprachenunterricht 6/1999, pp. 424 – 429

Frost, R. *Creating a Class Play.*
2007 | British Council website, www.teachingenglish.org.uk/think/literature/using_plays.shtml

G

Galloway, D. (ed.) *Selected Writings of Edgar Allan Poe. Poems, Tales, Essays and Reviews.*
1980 | Harmondworth: Penguin

Gehring, W. *Shakespeare auch an der Hauptschule? Warum nicht?*
1997 | In: Der Fremdsprachliche Unterricht Englisch, 6/1997, pp. 16 – 19

Gibson, R. *Teaching Shakespeare.*
1998 | Cambridge: Cambridge University Press

Grabe, W.
Stoller, F. *Teaching and Researching Reading*
2002 | Harlow: Pearson Education

Grabes, H. *Fiktion – Imitation – Ästhetik. Was ist 'Literatur'?*
1981 | Tübingen: Deutsches Institut für Fernstudien

H

Habib, M. *A History of Literary History.*
2005 | Oxford: Blackwell

Hallet, W.
Hebel, U. *Staging Women's Lives.*
2007 | In: Der Fremdsprachliche Unterricht Englisch, 1/2007, pp. 4 – 8

Harm, A. *My Short Science-Fiction-Horror-Love-Adventure Short Story.*
1997 | Englisch betrifft uns 4/1997, pp. 27 – 29

Hermes, L. *'Fun Reading': Möglichkeiten und Anregungen.*
1984 | In: Praxis des Neusprachlichen Unterrichts, 1984, pp. 115 – 123

Hesse, M. *Jugendliteratur als Schreiblehre.*
2002 | Tübingen: Narr

Hinz, K. *Schüleraktivierende Methoden im fremdsprachlichen Literaturunterricht.* 1996 | In: Praxis, 1996, pp.139 – 150

Holtwisch, H. *Kreative Textarbeit im Fremdsprachenunterricht und die Bewertung kreativ-orientierter Klassenarbeiten.* 1999 | In: Fremdsprachenunterricht 6/1999, pp. 417 – 424

Huck, C. *Children's Literature in the Elementary School.* 2001 | New York: McGraw-Hill

Hunt, P. *International Companion Encyclopedia of Children's Literature.* 1996 | London: Routledge

Hutcheon, L. *A Theory of Parody: The Teachings of Twentieth-Century Art Forms.* 1985 | New York: Methuen

J

Jakobson, R. Ihwe, J. (ed.) *Linguistik und Poetik.* 1971 | Literaturwissenschaft und Linguistik, Frankfurt/M.: Athenäum, pp. 512 – 548

Jarfe, G. *Die Sonette.* 2005 | In: Petersohn, R./Volkmann, L. (ed.), Shakespeare didaktisch II, Tübingen: Stauffenburg, pp. 269 – 284

Jeffcoate, R. *How Should We Teach Shakespeare's Plays?* 2002 | In: Der Fremdsprachliche Unterricht Englisch, 2/2002, pp. 11 – 13

Johnson, K. *An Introduction to Foreign Language Learning and Teaching.* 2001 | Harlow: Longman

K

Kamp, W. *Shakespeare im Film.* 2006 | In: Petersohn, R./Volkmann, L. (ed.), Shakespeare didaktisch I, Tübingen: Stauffenburg, pp. 119 – 134

Kieweg, W. *Creative writing.* 2003 | In: Unterrichts-Materialien Englisch 748E-04/2003, pp. 1 – 61

Klippel, F. *Englisch in der Grundschule.*
2000 | Berlin: Cornelsen

Klose, H. (ed.) *Shakespeare medial.*
2000 | Themenheft Der Fremdsprachliche Unterricht Englisch, 4/2000

Kramsch, C. *Context and Culture in Language Teaching.*
1993 | Oxford: Oxford University Press

Krashen, S. *The Power of Reading.*
1993 | Englewood: Libraries Unlimited

L

Ladousse, G. *Role Play.*
1987 | Oxford: Oxford University Press

Lorch, S. *Metaphor, Metaphysics, and MTV.*
1988 | In: Journal of Popular Culture, 22-3/1988, pp. 143 – 155

Ludwig, H.-W. *Arbeitsbuch Lyrikanalyse.*
1994 | Tübingen: Narr

M

Maley, A. *Short and Sweet.*
1995 | Cambridge: Cambridge University Press

Maley, A. / Duff, A. *Drama Techniques in Language Learning.*
1982 | Cambridge: Cambridge University Press

Martin, R. / Koch, P. *The Strongest of Them All.*
2000 | Berlin: Cornelsen

Meyer, M. *Schüler als Regisseure und Lehrer von 'A Midsummer Night's Dream'.*
1997 | In: Praxis des Neusprachlichen Unterrichts 2/1997, pp. 126 – 134

Mieder, W. *American Proverbs: A Study of Texts and Contexts.*
1989 | New York: Lang

Müller-Zettelmann — *Lyrik und Metalyrik. Theorie einer Gattung und ihrer Selbstbespiegelung anhand von Beispielen aus der englisch- und deutschsprachigen Dichtkunst.*
2000 | Heidelberg: Winter

Murray, C. (ed.) — *Encyclopedia of Literary Critics and Criticism.*
1999 | London: Routledge

N

Nuenning, A. — *Literatur ist, wenn das Lesen wieder Spaß macht.*
1997 | In: Der Fremdsprachliche Unterricht Englisch 3/1997, pp. 4 – 8

Nuenning, A. — *Von 'Teaching Drama' zu 'Teaching Plays'.*
1998 | In: Der Fremdsprachliche Unterricht Englisch 1/1998, pp. 4 – 10

Nuenning, A., Nuenning, V. — *An Introduction to the Study of English and American Literature.*
2004 | Stuttgart: Klett

P

Petersohn, R., Volkmann, L. (ed.) — *Shakespeare didaktisch*, I und II.
2005/2006 | Tübingen: Stauffenburg

R

Rau, A. — *Short Texts in Action – More Than Action in the Classroom!*
1999 | In: Der Fremdsprachliche Unterricht Englisch 6/1999, pp. 4 – 9

Rotter, W., Bendl, H. — *Your Companion to English Literary Texts*, vol. 1,
1981 | München: Manz

Rotter, W., Bendl, H. — *Your Companion to English Literary Texts*, vol. 2,
1984 | München: Manz

S

Savignon, S. — *Communicative Language Teaching for the Twenty-First Century.*
In: Celce-Murcia, M. (ed.), Teaching English as a Foreign Language, Boston: Heinle & Heinle, pp. 13 – 28

Scheller, I. — *Erfahrungsbezogener* Unterricht
1981 | Königstein: Scriptor

Schroeder-Thürauf — *Shakespeare vor der Oberstufe.*
2006 | In: Petersohn, S. R./Volkmann, L. (ed.), Shakespeare didaktisch I, Tübingen: Stauffenburg, 2006, pp. 197 – 206

Schuenke, C. — *Die Sonette. Zweisprachige Ausgabe.*
1999 | München: dtv

Sherman, J. — *Using Authentic Video in the Language Classroom.*
2003 | Cambridge: Cambridge University Press

stempleski, S. / Tomalin, B. — *Film.*
2001 | Oxford: Oxford University Press

Stredder, J. — *Shakespeare spielen – das Klassenzimmer als Bühne.*
2006 | In: Petersohn, R./Volkmann, L. (ed.), Shakespeare didaktisch I, Tübingen: Stauffenburg, pp. 21 – 42

Surkamp, C. / Nünning, A. — Englische Literatur unterrichten.
2006 | Seelze: Kallmeyer

T

Taubenböck, A. — *'If It Ain't a Pleasure, It Ain't a Poem': Lyrik – eine Gattung, die begeistern kann.*
2004 | In: Der Fremdsprachliche Unterricht Englisch, 67/2004, pp. 4 – 9

Taubenböck, A. — *Sonette und ihre Übersetzungen.*
2006 | In: Petersohn, R./Volkmann, L. (ed.), Shakespeare didaktisch I, Tübingen: Stauffenburg, pp. 183 – 196

Tendel, K. — *Eine Reihe Märchen.*
2007 | What's New, Spring 2007, Berlin: Cornelsen

Thaler, E. — *Musikvideoclips im Englischunterricht. Phänomenologie, Legitimität, Didaktik und Methodik eines neuen Mediums.*
1999 | München: Langenscheidt-Longman

Thaler, E. — *DVD im Englischunterricht.*
2001 | In: Der Fremdsprachliche Unterricht Englisch, 53/2001, pp. 40 – 41

THALER, E. *'I quote others only in order the better to express myself' – Aphorismen als Lernzünder.*
2004 | In: Der Fremdsprachliche Unterricht Englisch, 67/2004, pp. 36 – 41

THALER, E. *Henry James Meets Sting. Ein literarisch-multimediales Unterrichtsprojekt.*
2005 | In: Thaler, E./Schocker-von Ditfurth, M. (ed.). I too sing America. Perspectives on America. Perspektiven auf Amerika, Freiburg: Meisterdruck-Verlag, pp. 37 – 45

THALER, E. *Frieda meets Jura. A Short Cross-Cultural Short Story.* In: Doff, S. (ed.).
2006 | Festschrift des interdisziplinären wissenschaftlichen Nachwuchses für Diethelm und Friederike Klippel, München: Eigendruck, pp. 4 – 7

THALER, E. *Film-Based Language Learning.*
2007 | In: PRAXIS Fremdsprachenunterricht, 1/2007a, pp. 9 – 14

THALER, E. *Schulung des Hör-Seh-Verstehens.*
2007 | In: PRAXIS Fremdsprachenunterricht, 4/2007b, pp. 14 – 19

THALER, E. (ED.) *The New Summit. Lehrwerk für die Oberstufe.*
2007 | Paderborn: Schöningh

THALER, E. *Internet-Videos – Fremdsprachenlernen für die YouTube-Generation.*
2008 | In: PRAXIS Fremdsprachenunterricht 1/2008, 14 – 18.

THALER, E. *Das Lit-Lied. Literatur & Musik im Fremdsprachenunterricht.*
2009a | In: PRAXIS Fremdsprachenunterricht, 2, pp. 30 – 34

THALER, E. *Teaching Literature via Web 2.0.*
2009b | In: Eckstein, L./Reinfandt, C. (ed.), Anglistentag 2008 Tübingen. Proceedings, Trier: WVT, pp. 309 – 316

THALER, E. *Literaturunterricht im Zeitalter von Web 2.0.*
2011 | In: Thaler, Engelbert et al. (ed.), Foreign Language Teaching – History, Theory, Methodology (MAFF 25), München: Langenscheidt, pp. 159 – 165

THALER, E. *Englisch unterrichten.*
2012 | Berlin: Cornelsen

Thaler, E. *Teaching English with Films.*
2014 | Paderborn: UTB

Thaler, E. *Kurzprosa im Unterricht.*
2015 | In: Praxis Fremdsprachenunterricht, 1, pp. 7 – 9

Toolan, M. *Narrative: A Critical Linguistic Introduction.*
2001 | London: Routledge

U

Ur, P. *A Course in Language Teaching.*
1996 | Cambridge: Cambridge University Press

V

Volkmann, L. *'Phantasie ist wichtiger als Wissen': Ein Plädoyer für den Einsatz von Lyrik.*
1998 | In: Der Fremdsprachliche Unterricht Englisch, 33/1998, pp. 4 – 13

W

Wagner, H.P. *A History of British, Irish and American Literature.*
2003 | Trier: WVT

Werlich, E. *The Learner's Vocabulary for Text Analysis.*
1999 | Berlin: Cornelsen

Wessels, C. *Drama.*
1987 | Oxford: Oxford University Press

Wilkening, M. *SchülerInnen entwickeln dramatische Formen in offenen Unterrichtsphasen.*
1998 | In: Der Fremdsprachliche Unterricht Englisch 31/1998, pp. 16 – 20

Wright, A. *Storytelling with Children.*
1995 | Oxford: Oxford University Press

Z

Zapf, H. (Hg.) *Amerikanische Literaturgeschichte.*
1997 | Weimar: Metzler

Sachregister